Famous Parents of the Bible

FAMOUS
PARENTS
OF THE
BIBLE

Brian L. Harbour

BROADMAN PRESS
Nashville, Tennessee

Scriptures marked NASB are from the *New American Standard Bible.*
Copyright © The Lockman Foundation, 1960, 1962, 1963, 1971, 1972,
1973, 1975. Used by permission.

Scriptures marked RSV are from the Revised Standard Version of the
Bible, copyrighted 1946, 1952, © 1971, 1973.

Verses marked TLB are taken from *The Living Bible.* Copyright ©
Tyndale House Publishers, Wheaton, Illinois, 1971. Used by permission.

Dedicated
to
my children,
Jay,
Collin,
Cara, and
Marty,
who have taught me what I know about
parenting and who remind me every day
of how much I still don't know.

Preface

As a parent, I can sympathize with Charlie Shedd's story about his changing approach to parenting. Before he was married, he had an excellent lecture entitled "How to Raise Your Children." When he became involved with families who had children, he changed his lecture to "Some Suggestions to Parents." After he was married, the Shedds' first child came. Then, his lecture became "Feeble Hints to Fellow Strugglers." When the rest of his children came, he stopped giving the lecture altogether![1] Advice on parenting is difficult to give but is desperately needed in our day.

Much is being written and said today about marriage. Marriage enrichment retreats are popular. Several national organizations for family enrichment have been established. Husbands and wives who want help may draw on abundant resources.

A call from a mother of a twenty-three-year-old son who was on drugs and out of control reminded me: Where families are really hurting today is in the area of parent-child relationships. Much of the breakdown in the husband-wife relationship is precipitated or aggravated by a breakdown in the parent-child relationship. At that point we need assistance.

Where can we go for help? For the Christian, the Bible is our basic source book of information and inspiration. As in my books *Famous Couples of the Bible* and *Famous Singles of the Bible,* in this book I go to the Bible itself to draw out examples of biblical parents who can speak to us today through both their successes and failures.[2]

This book, *Famous Parents of the Bible,* will complete a trilogy on the family. In a day when we need help in parenting, the Word of God speaks to us with relevance and insight. Each of these three volumes has been structured so you may enjoy them privately *or* in groups. I have heard from many churches who have used *Famous Couples of the Bible* and *Famous Singles of the Bible* with groups.

These principles have guided me in writing this book.

First, I have tried to be *realistic.* Sometimes we so idealize family life that we leave no room for the normal difficulties of interpersonal relationships between parents and children.

Whenever there are babies in the home, there is going to be occasional chaos. One father chuckled to his wife, as they were crawling around in the baby's room picking up all his toys which were strewn from one corner to the other, "Now I know what Paul meant when he said, 'When I became a man, I put away childish things' " (1 Cor. 13:11).

Whenever there are children in the home, there are going to be problems of behavior. Over a cup of coffee, one neighbor asked the other, whose wild child had just entered the first grade, "Did Johnny cry when he went to school this morning?" The mother answered, "No, but the teacher did."

Whenever there are teenagers in the home, there is going to be a generation gap. One father was in dreadful anguish as he commented to his friend, "I finally talked my son into cutting his hair, and I'm sorry I did. Now I can see his earrings!"

A lady dragging five children onto a bus was asked by the bus driver, "Are those all yours, or is this a picnic?" She retorted, "They're all mine, and it ain't no picnic." Parenting is no picnic. Things are not always ideal in the home. We have to be realistic about the problems.

Second, I have attempted to be *practical.* Our greatest need is not declarations about *what* to do but also instructions on *how* to do it. I have attempted to include practical suggestions in each chapter.

Third, I have attempted to be *biblical*. This book is not about how my wife and I are parenting. These are not patterns or programs we have discovered. Our shortcomings and struggles as parents are as evident as are yours. Rather, this book is about *biblical* characters from whom we can derive *biblical* principles. Sometimes, we will be instructed by the failures of these biblical parents. At other times we will be inspired by the successes of these biblical parents. This needs to be remembered: the Bible is our guidebook for Christian parenting.

A special word of thanks to my wife Jan with whom I share the challenging adventure of parenthood.

BRIAN L. HARBOUR

Notes

1. Charlie Shedd, *You Can Be a Great Parent!* (Waco: Word Books, 1970), p. 7.

2. Brian L. Harbour, *Famous Couples of the Bible* (Nashville: Broadman Press, 1979); *Famous Singles of the Bible* (Nashville: Broadman Press, 1980).

Contents

Contents

1
The Providing Parent
Abraham
Genesis 21—22

Patrick Henry surely was one of our greatest early American statesmen. He delivered a dramatic speech in "The Parson's Cause" in 1763 which brought relief to the clergy of his day. His moving oration led to the adoption of the Virginia Resolution in 1765. He pushed Virginia toward military preparedness for the revolutionary war with his daring declaration, "I know not what course others may take, but, as for me, give me liberty or give me death."

Of all the statements Patrick Henry ever made, though, none is so eternally relevant as the explanation he gave about the disposition of his estate. On that matter he said,

> I have now disposed of all my property to my family. There is one thing more I wish I could give them, and that is the Christian religion. If they had that, and I had not given them one shilling, they would have been rich; and if they had not that, and I had given them all the world, they would be poor.[1]

What is it that you would most like to give to your children? An expansive estate, an inheritance, a well-established business, a noble name, or a godly heritage? Patrick Henry felt that nothing would be more valuable to give his children than a godly heritage.

In Genesis 21—22, we read about a parent of yesteryear who evidently agreed. His name was Abraham. He provided well for his son Isaac, but his most significant contribution was a godly heritage.

Becoming Isaac's father in the first place was not easy for Abraham. Many years passed before Isaac was finally born. How many years we do not know for certain. Twenty-five years had passed from the time Abraham left Haran until the time Isaac was born (Gen. 12:4; 21:5). The time of waiting for his son probably extended well back into the silent years before God communicated with Abraham at Haran. So it could have been sixty years or more!

Then, when the child came, the challenge of parenthood confronted Abraham. In chapters 21 and 22 of Genesis, we see that Abraham fulfilled God's charge "to keep the way of the Lord by doing righteousness and justice" (Gen. 18:19, RSV). In so doing, Abraham gave us two parenting patterns that we need to duplicate in the home today.

Presented an Identity

Abraham's first gift to Isaac was a personal identity. Genesis 21:4 says, "Abraham circumcised his son Isaac when he was eight days old, as God had commanded him" (RSV).

Often we skip over the idea of circumcision either because of our embarrassment in talking about it or because of our acceptance of circumcision as a common hygiene practice today. To skip over this idea, however, is to miss one of the keenest insights into parenting that Abraham provides.

Circumcision was widely practiced in antiquity, and many suggestions are given as to the reason for its origin. Some suggest that it began for physical reasons—as an aid to general cleanliness and hygiene. Others say that it was a form of sacrifice. It represented either a sacrifice of the reproductive powers to a fertility deity, or it was a substitute for human sacrifice, a part of the body being sacrificed in lieu of the whole. Others feel that it was an act of initiation, either into membership in the tribe or into manhood.

We are not left to speculate, though, about the reason for its origin in Israel. God told Abraham, "You shall be circumcised in the flesh of your foreskins, and it shall be a sign of the covenant between me and you" (Gen. 17:11, RSV).

The Book of Jubilees, a Jewish book dating from the second century BC, said that every child not circumcised "belongs not to the children of the covenant which the Lord made with Abraham, but to the children of destruction; nor is there, moreover, any sign on him that he is the Lord's" (15:26). Circumcision was a mark of identity for the covenant people of God.

When Abraham circumcised Isaac, then, he was saying to his son, "This is who you are, Isaac. You are an individual who has worth and value because of the elective grace of God. You are a part of the covenant people, God's forever family, a family of faith in which you can be loved and accepted and cared for." Abraham was helping Isaac to establish his identity.

There is no greater challenge in parenting than to help our children establish their identity, to determine who they are, and in the context of that understanding to decide what they want to do with their lives. Elizabeth O'Connor, in her book *The Eighth Day of Creation,* says that helping a child find a strong, clear feeling of personal identity is the definitive parental gift, the gift which entitles one to call himself a parent.[2]

This matter of personal identity is, of course, very complex. Several conclusions, however, seem to be obvious.

1. *A strong sense of personal identity is vital to healthy living.*

The failure to develop an identity leads to what Erik Erikson calls "identity diffusion."[3] This identity diffusion syndrome is revealed in several ways. Often this identity diffusion is seen in negative identity, that is, the attempt by a person to be what his family or immediate social group does not want him to be. The hippie movement was a clear expression of this. One man defined a hippie as a Joe who looks like a Jane and smells like a John. Hippies were young people who rebelled against the image of their parents and the identity their parents expected them to portray.

Identity diffusion is also revealed in extreme forms of self-consciousness, when a person is inordinately concerned with what other people think. It can lead to work paralysis as well. In this case, identity diffusion is manifest in an inability or an unwillingness to work. Identity diffusion is being increasingly revealed in our day in sexual diffusion, that is, deviant sexual patterns such as homosexuality.

These manifestations which indicate the lack of a strong personal identity take the joy out of life and lead to confusion, emptiness, and despair. A person who does not know who he is, is not a happy person, for a strong sense of personal identity is vital to healthy living.

2. *The early years of our life are crucial in developing our personal identity.*

Don't fall into the trap of thinking that by the time a child is a year old all of his patterns for life have been set. The development of our identity goes on throughout our entire lives, and dramatic changes are possible at any point. Nevertheless, the early years are critical. This is the truth of that biblical proverb which goes, "Train up a child in the way he should go, and even when he is old he will not depart from it" (Prov. 22:6, RSV).

What this means is that parenting is a full-time responsibility which demands careful attention at each stage of the child's life. You cannot wait until your child becomes a teenager to start being a parent. Parenting should not begin at a point of crisis. Instead, positive parenting must begin the day you bring your child home from the hospital.

3. *Both parents are involved in the process of developing personal identity in a child.*

We are experiencing today "the effemination of American society" in which the influence of women on our children has become predominant. A boy, for instance, comes first under the influence of his mother. Then, when he is old enough, he may be left with a child-care service or a sitter, again being under the influence of women. He will go through most of his school years with women teachers. At college, he will look for a woman to marry, so she will be able to care for him and share his life with him all the rest of his days. In our day, the importance of the mother in particular and women in general in shaping the identity of our children is evident.

We do not need to de-emphasize the influence of a mother on her child. What needs to be reemphasized is that the role of the father is also important. A recent study by two psychologists concluded that fathers bring a special dimension to child care that women do not give because they respond differently to children than do women. A father is not, as Margaret Mead once said, "a biological necessity but a social accident." Nor is he merely a poor substitute for the mother. Rather, he provides a unique dimension to parenthood. The study referred to above showed that children cope better with unusual social situations and relate better to strangers—both signs of a strong personal identity—if the father is an involved parent.[4]

What these researchers discovered experimentally has also been exhibited historically. Following the Korean War, twenty-one GI's in prison camps elected to stay in enemy hands. An investigator discovered that nineteen of the twenty-one felt unwanted by their fathers or stepfathers. Eleven of the boys had lost their fathers at an early age. Their problem, in part, was the lack of an adequate father figure.[5]

This truth is also being revealed today relationally. One of the most perverse forms of identity diffusion in our day is homosexuality. Studies on the subject conclude that a strong relationship of a son with his father will practically preclude the possibility of homosexuality. A strong father figure is also important to a daughter, for many marital problems can be traced to the search by the wife for a "phantom father" who never really existed.

Experimentally, historically, and relationally the fact is clear. Fathers' input is important.

Dads, do not relegate the role of parenting to the mothers. You, too, have a role to play. You, too, must be an involved parent. Both fathers and mothers play a significant part in the development of a healthy identity in our children.

4. *Personal identity is developed in the context of love and acceptance.*

The key ingredient which enables a child to develop an identity is the security which comes from love and acceptance of his parents. This is an especially encouraging insight for you women without mates and for you mothers who have been delegated the major part of the parenting responsibility in your family. You can, to a large degree, make up for the lack of a strong father figure in your home by assuring your child that nothing he ever does will make him less than what he or she is—your son or your daughter. Assure your child that your love is irrevocable, inescapable, and forever! The security of that affection will provide the soil in which his or her personal identity can bloom.

This is why the circumcision of Isaac, described in Genesis 21:4, is so important. Because it indicates that from the very beginning of his life, Isaac was given a sense of identity in a context of love and acceptance that enabled him to discover who he really was. That's parenting at its best!

Provided an Illustration

Genesis 22 shows us something else about this famous father of antiquity named Abraham. Not only did he present Isaac with an identity, he also provided him with an illustration. He not only showed him who he was; Abraham also provided his son a living example of how he could become that. Not just by his words but also by his life, Abraham provided a pattern of living that Isaac could emulate.

Genesis 22 reveals a dilemma in Abraham's life. He was convinced that God wanted him to sacrifice his son. This son for whom he had waited for sixty years, this son who was the hope of the future for Israel, this son who was more than life itself to his parents—this son God told Abraham to sacrifice.

Much about this story is difficult for us to understand, but look at Genesis 22 and see Abraham's response. Verse 3 says that the next morning after he received this command from God, Abraham moved without delay in obedience to fulfill the command. Unspoken sorrow stabbed his soul, but no complaints issued from his lips as Abraham came to the place for the sacrifice. He prepared the altar, tied Isaac up, laid him on the wood, and raised the knife to do what God had commanded. Only then did God stop Abraham with the explanation that he had passed the test. He had proved his faith. Instead of his son, God provided an animal for the sacrifice.

What does this experience tell us about parenting? I want to suggest to you that by his example Abraham taught Isaac a lesson about faith that he would never forget. He taught Isaac that nothing is to be preferred to God, that man must be ready to sacrifice his dearest treasure in the service of God. God has top priority. Abraham did not just say that. He did not just believe that. He demonstrated it in his life! That was the noblest inheritance that Abraham gave to his son, and it was transmitted by the example of his life.

In Israel there was an ancient proverb which said, "The fathers have eaten sour grapes, and the children's teeth are set on edge" (Jer. 31:29). What did that mean? Not that God would personally curse the children for the misdeeds of their parents, not that an unholy hex would be passed on through the blood, but that the environment in which a child grows up will inevitably influence his character. What it means is that learning begins at home, not by inoculation, not by indoctrination, but by illustration. Children do learn what they live.

> If a child lives with criticism, he learns to condemn.
> If a child lives with hostility, he learns to fight.
> If a child lives with fear, he learns to be apprehensive.
> If a child lives with pity, he learns to be sorry for
>   himself.
> If a child lives with jealousy, he learns to feel guilty.
> If a child lives with encouragement, he learns to be
>   confident.
> If a child lives with tolerance, he learns to be patient.
> If a child lives with acceptance, he learns to love.
> If a child lives with honesty, he learns what truth is.
> If a child lives with friendliness, he learns that the
>   world is a nice place to live. (Author Unknown)

A child learns what he lives! What kind of lessons are you teaching your children by your example?

Jerry Clower, the Mississippi humorist, says in all seriousness, "Every child, every young man, ought to have the right to stand flatfooted and say, 'My papa was a godly man.' "[6] Can your child say that about you?

One year on Father's Day I preached a sermon about the kind of a dad that pleased God. The next week a young lady in the congregation wrote me a letter telling how she identified my sermon with her dad. She concluded with this paragraph, "I have a good solid concept of God as my Heavenly Father. And the reason I do is because of my earthly father. It's because of Daddy that I am able to love God and relate to Him as my father."

Every child has the right to be able to say that about his dad and his mother. Isaac certainly could. Because of the life that he lived, Abraham was able to put the hand of his son into the hand of God, in whom life is to be found. There is no greater gift that you could give your child than a daily life of faith.

In at least three dimensions, this example of faith needs to be demonstrated to our children.

1. In the Home

Someone has suggested, "If you ain't got religion in the home, you ain't got religion." Atrocious grammar but deep spiritual truth is found in that statement. In the intimacy of our home relationships we need to present a pattern of faith for our children.

How do we illustrate our faith? Listen to how one poet put it:

> A woman sat by a hearthside place
> Reading a book, with a pleasant face,
> Till a child came up, with a childish frown,
> And pushed the book, saying, "Put it down."
> Then the mother, slapping his curly head,
> Said, "Troublesome child, go off to bed;
> A great deal of Christ's life I must know
> To train you up as a child should go."
> And the child went off to bed to cry,
> And denounce religion—by and by.
> Another woman bent over a book,
> With a smile of joy and an intent look,
> Till a child came up and jogged her knee
> And said of the book, "Put it down—take me."
> Then the mother sighed as she stroked his head,
> Saying softly, "I never shall get it read;
> But I'll try by loving to learn His will,
> And His love into my child instill."
> That child went to bed without a sigh,
> And will love religion—by and by.[7]

Whether our children will desire faith or detest faith will be largely determined by how we act in the home.

2. In the Church

Some families go to church when they feel like it, when they have nothing else to do, when they have the right clothes, when they do not have company coming in, and when they are in town. Church attendance is low on their list of priorities.

These parents fail to illustrate their faith by active involvement in the life of the church. Then they wonder why their children never care about the church.

I have never known parents who were having a positive, spiritual influence on their children who were not at the same time actively involved in some church or religious group.

Judge Allen Ardell of Iowa once said, "The Juvenile Court considers religious training of such prime importance in the determination of the cause of delinquency and the possibility of rehabilitation, that one of the first matters inquired into is the children's attendance at Sunday School and church attendance by the parents."[8]

Whether our children will embrace faith or evade faith will be determined by our involvement in the church.

3. *In the World*

Our children must not only see our faith demonstrated at home and in the church; they must also see our faith demonstrated in the world.

A family in Canada had ten children. Of these, six are serving on some foreign mission field. The other four children are active Christians at home, and they support the "overseas branch." Someone asked these children what it was about their parents that had such an influence on their lives. They gave many answers. The one which repeatedly surfaced was their explanation that their parents "lived the way they talked."

What a heritage to give our children!

Notes

1. Robert J. Hastings, *My Money and God* (Nashville: Broadman Press, 1961), pp. 95-96.

2. Elizabeth O'Connor, *The Eighth Day of Creation* (Waco: Word Books, 1971), p. 78.

3. Erik H. Erikson, "The Syndrome of Identity Diffusion in Adolescents

and Young Adults," in *Discussions on Child Development* (New York: International Universities Press, 1958), 3:153.

4. John W. Drakeford, *Wisdom for Today's Family* (Nashville: Broadman Press, 1978), p. 103.

5. Ibid.

6. Jerry Clower, *Ain't God Good!* (Waco: Word Books, 1975), p. 32.

7. Anonymous, quoted in David Edens, *Why God Gave Children Parents* (Nashville: Broadman Press, 1966), p. 48.

8. Walter B. Knight, ed. *Knight's Treasury of Illustrations* (Grand Rapids: Wm. B. Eerdmans Publishing Co., 1963), p. 248.

2
The Problem Parents
Isaac and Rebekah
Genesis 25:19-28

This intriguing story of Isaac's children begins with the rift between the two brothers when Esau sold his birthright and ends with his reconciliation with Jacob many years later. The story, which covers about nine chapters in the Book of Genesis, provides interesting insight into family life at its worst. The home of Isaac and Rebekah was one plagued with problems. It is like many homes in our day.

The home today has become for many parents and children not a place of blessedness and joy but a hell on earth. The generation gap has cut a ragged edge across society. Much of the crisis in the home has been precipitated by a breakdown in the relationship between parent and child and by an accompanying failure on the part of parents to fulfill their God-given responsibility of parenthood.

The story of Isaac and Rebekah reminds us that this is not solely a modern-day phenomenon. In the midst of God's chosen people, in this special family through whom God would carry out his plan of redemption, we also see evidences of parental failure.

What did Isaac and Rebekah do wrong?

The Seriousness of the Responsibility

Failure began for Isaac and Rebekah when they did not realize the seriousness of their responsibility as parents, the seriousness of the obligation when a child comes into the home.

They certainly wanted a child. Even today, the desire of most new families is to have a child, adding joy to their home, but having a child was of special significance in the Old Testament period for two reasons. For one thing, with the concept of an afterlife not yet fully developed, they thought the only way that a person's life could be perpetuated was through his child. When a man was buried that would be the end of his name unless his life could be continued and his name carried forward by a son. A second reason that Isaac and Rebekah most certainly wanted a child was that, in this period of time, childbearing was evidence of God's blessing on your life and marriage. Barrenness was a sign of God's disfavor. So, Isaac and Rebekah deeply desired to have a child.

Notice that they not only wanted a child; they also patiently waited for the child. Twenty years passed between their marriage and the birth of their twin sons. Many times during those twenty years they must have cried themselves to sleep at night with the agonizing embarrassment of their childlessness. How patient Isaac and Rebekah were.

When Abraham and Sarah could not have a child, Abraham went in to his concubine and had a son named Ishmael. Abraham and Sarah could not wait for God to work it out in his own way. None of that impetuous impatience is seen in Isaac and Rebekah.

In addition to their desire and their patience, their infinite qualifications for parenthood seem obvious. If ever there were a marriage made in heaven, this was it. Rebekah was a young girl with the right background. She came from a good family and was adequately trained. Her role as Isaac's wife was carefully worked out according to the intricacies of God's plan. Isaac was the son of the father whose faith was proclaimed even in the New Testament and who came to be known as the father of the Hebrew people. This was no last-minute arrangement, a couple capriciously thrown together in the eleventh hour, but a marriage of two special people culminated after a period of careful search and divine leadership.

Yet, despite all their qualifications, their patient waiting, and their burning desire for a child, when the children came, Isaac and Rebekah revealed by their actions that they were not prepared to fulfill the responsibility.

What a joy it is to have a new child placed in your hands and to know that the child is yours, to see flesh of your flesh and bone of your bone, six or seven (or ten!) pounds of red, screaming humanity that will someday become a man or a woman. Of all the wonderful blessings of life I have known, at the top of the list is that excitement I felt when first Jay and then Collin and then Cara and then Marty came into our lives. Home from the hospital we came to begin the joyous experience of parenthood. There is no joy in the world like the precious privilege of parenthood.

On the other hand, to see a child whose malleable life has been twisted out of shape, to see girls or boys who have imposed on their inner souls handicaps which the finest skill of trained counselors cannot remove, to see these God-given blessings of life sacrificed by the ineptness and stupidity and preoccupation and busyness and smother love of parents— that is one of life's greatest tragedies.

Because of the far-reaching consequences of parental failure, no responsibility in life compares to that given to parents to mold and develop the lives of their children. How we need to rediscover the truth of what Chrysostom said sixteen centuries ago: "Higher than every painter, higher than every sculptor and than all artists do I regard him who is skilled in the art of forming the soul of children."[1]

What shapes the lives of our children? What determines their destinies? Some claim that heredity most often determines what a child is to become. Other experts state that environment is the primary factor which sets the pattern of the child's life. Whichever is true, the awesome fact is: We parents are responsible for providing both! Heredity and environment are both controlled by parents.

A cartoon showed a baby kangaroo peeking out of its mother's pouch. The caption stated, "Her mother determines her point of view!"

It's true. Parents determine the quality of home life in which the child is reared. Parents impress upon the mind of a child the proper order for the values of life. Parents give the children their first ideas about what life is like. Parents influence the child to feel that God is important or not important. Parents decide what objects for affection and attention are thrust upon their children. Parents basically determine the direction the children will go.

One of our worst faults today is the same one Isaac and Rebekah exhibited long ago: we fail to realize the seriousness of our responsibility as parents.

The Uniqueness of the Children

A second mistake is obvious in the story of Isaac and Rebekah. They did not allow their children to develop their own uniqueness.

How different were these two sons of Isaac.

Jacob and Esau had *different looks.* Esau was covered with so much reddish hair that the Bible seems to indicate one would think he was wearing a fur coat. Jacob, on the other hand, was smooth-skinned and fair.

Jacob and Esau had *different interests.* Esau, the Bible indicates, became a skillful hunter who enjoyed being out in the wilds of nature. Jacob, on the other hand, was a quiet sort who liked to stay at home.

These two brothers also had *different attitudes.* To Jacob, the ranking in the family and the privileges of the birthright were of ultimate importance. Esau, when he was hungry, would rather fill his stomach than have the privileges of the birthright. That day when he came home hungry he threw away his birthright for something to eat, and the Bible says, "He ate and drank and went on about his business, indifferent to the loss of the rights he had thrown away" (Gen. 25:34, TLB).

What a difference there was between these two boys, each one unique, each one having those distinct qualities that could be valuable if developed. The sad fact that permeates the entire narrative, however, is that Isaac and Rebekah did not accept the boys in their uniqueness. They did not love them as they were. Instead, they manipulated them. They tried to fit them into their own mold.

Early in the story the Bible records that Esau was Isaac's favorite because he brought him good things to eat. Jacob was Rebekah's favorite because he spent a great deal of time with her around the house. Each parent gravitated toward that son whose special interests pleased them.

When Esau at the age of forty decided to marry, Isaac and Rebekah did not approve. The Bible indicates that they were bitter about his marriage (Gen. 26:34-35). They didn't accept Esau's choice because they didn't really accept Esau.

When Isaac was preparing to give his final blessing to Esau his eldest son, Rebekah began her treacherous conniving. She didn't want Jacob to be left out, so she devised a plan and forced him to follow through on it.

From beginning to end, Rebekah and Isaac devised a mold and tried to force their children into it. It reminds me of the cartoon strip called *Momma*. The daughter said to her mother, "Momma, you don't approve of anything I do, where I go, who I see . . . why can't you let me do what I want?" To which the mother answered, "Darling, as long as I have but one life to live, I'm going to live yours."

That is a tragedy repeated in many families today. Too many parents try to live the lives of their children instead of allowing them to develop their unique talents and fulfill the distinct destiny God has planned for them.

Two grandmothers were bragging about their grandchildren. One, quite impressed, asked the other, "How old are your grandsons?" "Well," she replied, "the doctor is two, and the lawyer is four!"

How often parents and grandparents alike set goals for their children, determine their destinies, and then force them into those parental patterns. Actually, your child might not want to be a doctor. He may prefer to be a plumber. He might not be called of God to be a preacher; he might be called to be an outstanding Christian layman. He might not be made to be a football player; he might be made to play the clarinet in the band.

One counselor has observed that the primary role of the family is that of liberation. The task lasts from the day we bring our new baby through the front door until the day he walks out that door to face life on his own. We are to liberate our children to be the persons God created them to be.

Charles Swindoll provides an interesting insight from the familiar parental proverb in Proverbs 22:6. He points out that the verse says, "Train up a child *in*." The term *in* means "in keeping with" or "in cooperation with" or "in accordance to." The *New American Standard Bible* has this marginal note, "according to his way." The challenge of parenthood is not to train your child in the way you want him to go. Instead, our challenge is to observe our child so that we can discover *his* way, and then adapt our training accordingly.[2]

Every child is different. Each of our children is unique. We have two who live to eat and two who eat to live. We have one who is intricately organized and neat and one who is the opposite. We have one with blonde hair and three who are brunets. Each child is different!

Your child was not created to be a carbon copy of yourself. Your child was not made to fit your mold. Your child is a unique individual with singular talents and a distinct destiny. Much of today's misery comes from individuals who have been diverted from their original destiny by parents who tried to fit them into a predetermined mold. How like Isaac and Rebekah many parents are today.

The Importance of Positive Spiritual Influence

There is yet a third mistake that Isaac and Rebekah made. They failed to give positive spiritual direction to their children.

Isaac and Rebekah had so much going for them. They had such a rich heritage. They were so imminently prepared and qualified. Yet, in the one area above all else with which they should have been concerned, they failed; for they refused to be the spiritual leaders of their home.

When we see the ultimate consequences of that failure—the bitter enmity between the two brothers; the cleavage in the family; the bitter disappointment of Isaac; the agonizing anguish of Esau; the separation of Rebekah and her beloved son Jacob so that she never had the privilege of seeing him again; and the transformation of the sensitive, beautiful young Rebekah pictured in 24:15-16 into the dejected, disappointed mother living under the shadow of her own evil scheming that we see in chapter 27—when we see all that we realize what a destructive force is let loose when parents refuse to give positive spiritual direction to their home.

Someone has compared the descendants of two men who lived in early America. One was a devout Christian minister whose name was Jonathan Edwards. He married a consecrated Christian girl, and out of their union, over a certain period of years, came 729 descendants. Of these 300 were ministers, sixty-five were college professors, thirteen were university presidents, sixty were authors of good books, three were US congressmen, and one was vice-president of the United States. Almost 70 percent of them made a positive contribution to society, and there was only one known "black sheep" in the family.

The other man was an unbeliever named Max Jukes. He lived close to Jonathan Edwards, in the same period of time. However, he did not believe in God. He married an unbeliever, and they produced over that same period of time 1,026 descendants, 300 of whom died early in life. One hundred went to prison for an average of thirteen years each. Two hundred were public prostitutes. Another 100 were alcoholics. The family cost the state over one million dollars, and none made any significant contribution to society.

What was the difference? Why one family with so rich a heritage and the other with so little good produced? The primary factor is that in one family the parents dared to be spiritual leaders of their home.

Your family can go either way. Your family can be like that of Jonathan Edwards or like that of Max Jukes. What will determine the direction in which your family goes is your ability to avoid the mistakes of Isaac and Rebekah. Recognize the seriousness of your parental responsibility. Accept the uniqueness of your children. Give spiritual leadership to your home. Then you can avoid perpetuating the pattern of these problem parents of the past.

Notes

1. Walter B. Knight, ed., *Knight's Treasury of Illustrations* (Grand Rapids: Wm. B. Eerdmans Publishing Co., 1963), p. 25.

2. Charles R. Swindoll, *You & Your Child* (New York: Bantam Books, 1980), p. 7.

3
The Practical Parent
Manoah
Judges 13:2-8

The term *planned parenthood* brings to mind the matter of birth control. The kind of "planned parenthood" about which we should be more concerned is child control. The real challenge facing the family today is not planning to prevent children from being born but planning to take care of them after they are here.

Parenthood is one of the most enigmatic undertakings of life. We spend nine months wondering when our children will get here and then the rest of their lives wondering where they have gone. We spend the first few years wondering when they will turn in. Then, we spend the rest of their lives wondering how they will turn out. We spend the first few months teaching our children to walk and talk. Then we spend the next fifteen years telling them to sit down and be quiet. We spend half our time teaching our children. The other half of our time we are telling them not to be so smart!

Parenthood is not only an enigmatic undertaking but also an awesome responsibility. Parents are not just individuals who bear children, bore teenagers, and board newlyweds. Parents are individuals who largely determine the attitudes, outlooks, and philosophies of the children who are given into their care.

Ironically, the enigmatic, awesome task of parenthood is the only major job we tackle in life without previous training. It is life's greatest task. Yet, we are so inadequately prepared for it. That is why every parent needs to say what Manoah said in our text when he discovered he and his wife were going to have a child. "O Lord, I pray thee, let the man of God whom thou didst send come again to us, and teach us what we are to do with the boy that will be born" (Judg. 13:8, RSV). Manoah did not just want to know *that* he had a child coming. Nor was he overly concerned about *when* the child was coming. He wanted to know *what to do* with him after he got here.

The man of God or angel did return, and he informed Manoah that his son was to be a Nazirite. Read Numbers 6:1-8 for information about the Nazirite vow. To make a Nazirite vow meant to refuse to cut your hair, to abstain from wine, and to avoid contact with a dead body. At times the Nazirite vow was temporary and voluntary. At other times, it was permanent and imposed. In either case, the purpose of the Nazirite vow was to refrain from certain things in life so one could be more fully dedicated to God. But the specifics of his instructions are not recorded.

What else did the angel tell Manoah about his son? We are not sure, but on the basis of other passages throughout the Scriptures, let me surmise what the angel told Manoah and his wife.

Love Him

The first thing the angel might have told Manoah was: "Love this child. Whatever else you do, give your child a warm, caring environment in which to grow up." Children are a gift from God, the Bible teaches, and we are to love them. Some might think it is unnecessary to remind parents of this. It would be like telling a duck to swim or a bird to fly or a child to like candy.

To a degree, love is spontaneous for a parent. Most parents do love their children. Our problem comes in knowing how to express that love. How can we show our children we really love them?

1. *Words*

We can express our love with words. One husband commented to his wife, "Honey, I care for you so much it's all I can do to keep from telling you." That's the problem in too many homes, not only in husband-wife relationships but in parent-child relationships. We so seldom express what we really feel by saying, "Son, I love you," or "Honey, you are really special to me." Words can have a powerful, positive effect on our children.

2. *Time*

We can also express our love with our time. Everyone knows the blight of busyness. It is part of the fabric of our culture. If we are short on time, usually our family gets left out. No one has to fight this problem more than a preacher.

What can we do? Some experts suggest setting aside a family night each week that has top priority on everyone's schedule. Some suggest using mealtime for real sharing. Some suggest a time alone with each child by each parent at least once a month.

Different approaches will work for different people. In each approach, three factors seem evident. We will spend time with our children if we love them. Second, we will have to plan for this time. It won't just happen. Third, the amount of time is not as important as giving undivided attention during the time we have.

3. *Listening*

We can also express our love by listening. Most parents are good at lecturing but not listening. What we need is a two-way flow of words and ideas and feelings. Sometimes this is dangerous. One mother said, "My daughter tells me everything." And then she added, "And I'm a nervous wreck." Listening can be dangerous. However, we will not convince our children of our love unless we listen to them.

4. *Praise*

We can also express our love by praise. One of the purposes

of the home is to provide a sense of security for a child. Paul Tournier, in *A Place for You,* states that if a person finds a place or a community within his family—if he finds acceptance within his family—it will be easy for him to find other places throughout life.[1] As a parent you are in a position to encourage your child or discourage him, to build him up or tear him down, to liberate him or hang him up with inhibitions. If you really love your child, you will do everything you can to affirm that child and encourage him and give him a home base of security from which he can approach life.

Haim Ginott, in his classic work *Between Parent and Child,* states that praise can sometimes be unhealthy. In a lengthy discussion he develops this idea: "The single most important rule is that praise deal only with the child's efforts and accomplishments, *not* with his character and personality."[2]

Kevin Leman, in his book *Parenthood Without Hassles: Well Almost,* picks up this same theme. He declares, "Praise creates a pressure situation for children." He explains that praise "conveys to a child that he is praised because he did something so well, which in turn conveys to a child that he must always do that well in order to be held in high esteem."[3] Hence, the pressure.

Frankly, their distinction between praise for behavior and praise for personality is not clear. Every child needs to feel good about himself, not merely about his actions. Granted, we must not convey to our children that their worth is determined by their accomplishments. Nevertheless, praise about what our children do and about who they are, when carefully administered, is a healthy way to express our love.

There is no way to measure the life-sustaining force of a father's smile, a mother's tenderness, a word of encouragement, or a few uninterrupted minutes listening to a four-year-old expound on his four-year-old problems. There is no way to measure the power of love. But you can mark it down. Love properly expressed is the primary ingredient in planned parenthood.

Teach Him the Limits

Then the angel might have instructed Manoah, "You also need to teach your child the limits within which life is to be lived."

To love we must add discipline. Discipline, simply defined, is the method by which we teach our children the comfortable limits within which life is to be lived. Defining discipline is not as difficult as dispensing discipline. How to exert that discipline is not easily discerned.

No aspect of parenting evokes as much debate as this matter of discipline. The large number of spoiled brats who have been ruined under the method of permissiveness suggest the need for strong discipline. On the other hand, the epidemic of child abuse and child beating suggests the need for great care in administering that discipline.

Conflicting opinions persist. Several factors seem to emerge out of the conflict and confusion.

1. *Discipline is necessary.*

The Bible clearly teaches the need for discipline. In Proverbs 29:15-17, the Bible says, "Scolding and spanking a child helps him to learn. Left to himself, he brings shame to his mother. . . . Discipline your son and he will give you happiness and peace of mind" (TLB). Proverbs 22:6 says, "Train up a child in the way he should go." The word *train* means "to press in, to make narrow," that is, to set limits. According to the Bible, discipline is a necessary part of parenthood.

2. *Discipline and love are not antithetical.*

Some parents disavow discipline for their children because they claim to love them too much. Discipline, however, is not the opposite of love. It is the outcome of love. When we discipline our children, when we set limits for them, we are telling our children that they are worth enough not to be allowed to get into bad trouble. Many experts suggest that children derive their security from knowing where the boundaries are. Disciplining our children is one of the ways we can show them we really care.

3. *Discipline can be administered in many different ways.*

The Bible evidently teaches that spanking is one of the methods (Prov. 13:24; Prov. 22:15). Charlie Shedd, a well-known spokesman on the family, disagrees. Quoting a Chinese proverb, "He who strikes the first blow has run out of ideas," Shedd avows that spanking is not an acceptable means of administering discipline.[4]

I don't know what the Chinese think is best, but the Bible says, "He that spareth his rod hateth his son" (Prov. 13:24). There are times when one of the best disciplinary methods is to pat our children on the back—often enough, hard enough, and low enough.

There are, of course, other methods of discipline.

The law of reinforcement is a method suggested by James Dobson. Dobson refers to the law of reinforcement as "the most magnificent theory ever devised for the control of behavior." Simply stated, the law of reinforcement says, "Behavior which achieves desirable consequences will recur." By rewarding acceptable behavior and refusing to award unacceptable behavior, our children can be taught the limits within which they are to live their lives.[5]

Charles Swindoll recommends what he calls "disciplining with dignity." Disciplining with dignity involves two dimensions that Swindoll finds repeatedly suggested in Proverbs: *yahsaar* and *yahkaag*. Yahsaar (Prov. 13:24) is translated "discipline," and it involves correction administered to one's child. The rod, says Swindoll, is the instrument by which that correction is to be administered. *Yahkaag* is translated reproof, and it involves instruction given to the child. Swindoll explains, "*Yahsaar* has to do with the outside, the outer activity, the outer wrong, the outer overt disobedience. *Yahkaag* deals with the inside. It supplies information and direction." Put correction and instruction together, and you have "disciplining with dignity."[6]

Whichever turns you on, the point is that there are many ways to discipline our children.

4. *Our discipline must be consistent.*

When our children know what the rules are, when these rules are applied with consistency, and when the parents stand together in administering them, then discipline can be a positive learning experience in the life of our children.

5. *Discipline must lead to self-discipline.*

Our discipline must never be merely a punishment for an action or a ventilation of our frustration. Rather, discipline should provide a learning experience by which our child learns what the limits are, so he may eventually be able to apply them to himself.

6. *Discipline must be given in the context of love.*

Charlie Shedd suggests that the final step of any experience of discipline in the home ought to be "Re-attachment." We must show our child that we still love him, that our disfavor has been toward his action and not toward him. We must communicate to him the fact that he can never do anything so dreadful or say anything so terrible or be anything so awful that we no longer love him.[7]

A child is not born with an inherent understanding of the limits within which life must be lived. He has to be taught. Therefore, one of the things the angel must have told Manoah was to teach his son the limits of life.

Put Him in Touch With God

At least one more suggestion might have been given by the angel to Manoah. "You also need to put your child in touch with God. Your child and God were made for each other. Do everything you can to get them together."

One of the promises Charlie Shedd made to his son Peter was: "*I will do everything I can to put your hand in the hand of your Heavenly Father.*"[8] What a promise! That means to pray for our children. That means to raise them in the church. That means to read the Bible to them. That means to set an example for them in church membership. That means to talk to them about the Lord. That means to be a spiritual example before them. That means to show them the Christian life is fun.

One father was sitting in the room of his dying son. Suddenly the father's emotions erupted, and the tears began to flow. The son soothed, "Don't cry Dad. When I die I'm going to heaven, and I will go right up to Jesus and tell him that it is because of you that I am there."[9]

What a thrill it would be to have all our children speak those words about us, to have every son and every daughter grateful because we put them in touch with God.

Conclusion

All kinds of suggestions are given on how to be a parent. Many of the suggestions are good and helpful. I believe that parental training ought to begin with the church; our resource person ought to be God; our book of instructions ought to be God's Word.

Like Manoah we need to cry out, "O, Lord, I pray thee, let the man of God whom thou didst send come again to us, and teach us what we are to do with the boy that will be born" (RSV). Then, we need to hear the Lord say to us, "That child is my special gift to you. Love him. Show him the limits in which life is to be lived. And put him in touch with me."

Notes

1. Quoted in Herbert Wagemaker, *Why Can't I Understand My Kids?* (Grand Rapids: Zondervan Publishing House, 1973), p. 67.

2. Haim Ginott, *Between Parent & Child* (New York: The MacMillan Co., 1965), p. 39.

3. Kevin Leman, *Parenthood Without Hassles: Well Almost* (Eugene: Harvest House Publishers, 1979), pp. 110-11.

4. Charlie Shedd, *Promises to Peter* (Waco: Word Books, 1970), p. 12.

5. James Dobson, *Dare to Discipline* (Wheaton: Tyndale House Publishers, 1970), p. 63.

6. Charles R. Swindoll, *You & Your Child* (New York: Bantam Books, 1980), pp. 87-95.

7. Shedd, *Promises to Peter,* p. 53.

8. Ibid., p. 15.

9. Clarence W. Kerr, *God's Pattern for the Home* (Los Angeles: Lowman Publishing Co., 1953), p. 83.

4
The Pious Parents
Hannah and Elkanah
1 Samuel 1:1-28

Psalm 127:3 declares, "Behold, children are a gift of the Lord;/The fruit of the womb is a reward./Like arrows in the hand of a warrior,/So are children of one's youth./How blessed is the man whose quiver is full of them" (NASB).

One author has paraphrased that Psalm to say instead, "Behold, children are a burden from the Lord; and the fruit of the womb must be his way of testing us. As the source of endless work and continued aggravation, so are the children of one's youth. Unhappy is the man who hears his neighbor ask, 'Do all these kids belong to you?' "[1]

What are children, a blessing or a burden? For Hannah, there was no doubt about how that question would be answered. To her, children were a blessing, a coveted reward from God, and the deepest desire of Hannah's heart was that she could have the privilege of giving birth to a child. First Samuel 1:10 captures the depth of her desire, "She was deeply distressed and prayed to the Lord, and wept bitterly." Life's greatest honor, in Hannah's estimation, was to be able to have a baby.

Many share that same desire today. Although a growing number of couples opt for a childless marriage, the hope which Hannah held is still shared by a majority of married couples. Someone has said, "Without children, no home is complete; with children, no home is intact." Those of us who have children can vouch for the veracity of the last half of the statement. Most couples without children would agree with the former half. They are convinced that life's greatest honor is to be able to give birth to a baby.

I believe they are wrong. Life's greatest honor is not to give birth to a child. Life's greatest honor is to raise the child God has given you in a manner that is pleasing to Him, to be parents who honor God.

How can that happen? I believe we have a good parental model in Hannah and Elkanah. Notice the elements in their home that enabled them to be successful parents.

Devotion

The first thought which struck me as I read the biblical story is the devotion Hannah and Elkanah had for each other.

We see evidence of this in verse 5. When Elkanah and his family went to worship at Shiloh, he gave to his wife and her sons and daughters something to offer in sacrifice. But to Hannah he gave "a double portion, for he loved Hannah" (NASB).

We see evidence of it again in verse 8. When he noticed the sadness of Hannah, Elkanah reminded her, "Am I not better to you than ten sons?" The exact meaning of that phrase is uncertain. The implication is that Elkanah treated Hannah with the greatest possible love and devotion.

Hannah's deep anguish over her childlessness was also an indication of her devotion for Elkanah. Because of her deep love for Elkanah she wanted to produce a child for him.

You may ask, "What does that have to do with parenting?" The answer is, "Everything." The quality of the relationship between a husband and wife will inevitably influence the children. If there is hostility in the husband-wife relationship, it will seep over onto the children. If there is alienation between a husband and a wife, it will cast a shadow of insecurity over the children. If, on the other hand, the husband-wife relationship is strong, if it is characterized by the kind of devotion Hannah and Elkanah had for each other, then that will create a sense of security, peace, and well-being in the lives of the children.

What does it take for a strong husband-wife relationship? Let me suggest six principles.

1. *Adaptability*

The first principle is adaptability. Where do we develop our image of what marriage is? Before we are married, how do we know what a husband or wife is supposed to do? Three sources form our basic understanding of marriage.

One is the home we grew up in. Our parents are the first models of husbands and wives we are exposed to. Good or bad, we learn from them. As we observe their relationships, their responses, and their roles, we develop a concept of what husbands and wives are supposed to be and do.

A second source of our understanding of marriage is what we see and read from outside sources. Every book we read, every magazine article we peruse, every movie we watch, every television show we view, and every family we observe feed us information concerning the role of a wife and husband in the home.

A third source of information about marriage is what our married friends tell us. As we approach the marrying age, many of our friends precede us into that relationship. As we talk with them, observe them, watch them, our understanding of marriage is further developed.

From these three different sources, our understanding of marriage and the roles of husband and wife is shaped. The problem is that no two people ever have the same exact concept. Many of the differences are worked out during the courtship period. However, we bring some of the different expectations and understandings into marriage with us. As one family expert puts it, "The grinding of the gears as they try to mesh in the early years is often very painful! What's involved is the difficult task of creating a workable synthesis of the legacies of the two childhoods which the partners bring into any marriage."[2]

Transforming "my" understanding of marriage and "your" understanding of marriage into "our" understanding of marriage is quite a challenge, and much conflict results. This conflict can be paralytic or catalytic. That is, it can destroy the relationship. Or it can be the stimulus, the catalyst, that brings about a deeper and richer relationship.

The truth is that this challenge is not just one which faces us in the early years of marriage but all the way through. At each stage, whether the challenges which face us are paralytic or catalytic will depend on our adaptability, our willingness to work together until we can find a mutually acceptable middle ground. Adaptability is the first key to a happy marriage.

2. *Association*

A second key is association. According to the earliest creation narrative, the purpose of marriage is that of companionship. Because God said it was not good for man to be alone, he created woman. She became the helpmate, the one who filled the relationship hunger which was a part of his being. Because companionship is the primary purpose of marriage, it naturally follows that one of the ways we can make our marriage what it ought to be is to spend time with each other.

Rodney Dangerfield, who always complains that he gets no respect, has no respect at home either. He jokingly said, "My wife and I sleep in separate rooms; we have dinner apart; we take separate vacations. We're doing everything we can to keep our marriage together." In reality, what most of us need to keep our marriages together is not more separation but more togetherness. This is especially urgent today because of the polarization of the family which living in our modern world causes. With both partners working in most cases and the children involved in numerous extracurricular activities, it is becoming truer and truer: Husbands and wives can live together all through the years, operate from the same house, raise a family together, and yet never make time to get to know each other!

If we are to have happy homes, we must find meaningful time with each other. Association, that's the second key.

3. *Affirmation*

A third principle of a happy marriage is affirmation. Not only should we spend more time together, we should learn to use that time to affirm each other.

Now, granted, there are some things in our lives that make affirmation difficult. One wife whose husband had been sick was asked by a concerned friend, "Is your husband all right now?" "Well," she replied, "He's not all right, but he's back like he was before."

Another young groom said to his wife, "Honey, I hope you don't mind if I point out a few of your faults." "Not at all," she responded. "It was those faults that kept me from getting a better husband."

Despite our evident human foibles, all of us have good qualities as well. Happy homes are those in which husbands and wives learn to see the positive in each other and affirm that.

4. *Allegiance*

A fourth principle of a happy marriage is allegiance.

Herman and Gertrude had been married only a week when they moved into their new home, a home which Gertrude paid for with her money. As they walked into their home for the first time, she turned to him and said, "Herman, if it were not for my money, we wouldn't be here." That afternoon the furniture was brought in, furniture which Gertrude paid for with her money. As the men put the furniture in place, she said to her husband, "Herman, if it were not for my money, this furniture wouldn't be here." The next day they delivered a beautiful color television, a television that Gertrude paid for with her money. As the television was turned on, Gertrude said,

"Herman, if it were not for my money, this television wouldn't be here." Finally, he responded. He said, "Gertrude, I don't want to make you feel too bad. But if it were not for your money, I wouldn't be here!"

What does keep us together? It's neither money, nor a certain feeling, nor common interests, nor the children, nor love. It is commitment.

I have numerous articles in my file about infidelity in marriage. Most of them analyze the reasons for infidelity. There is only one reason for infidelity, and that is a misunderstanding of the commitment of marriage. There is in the commitment of marriage an exclusiveness that demands absolute allegiance. When you get married, you have no right to give of yourself physically or emotionally to anyone else. Instead, you have an obligation to give yourself physically and emotionally to each other.

When a couple understands and accepts that absolute allegiance to each other, they are setting the foundation for a happy home.

5. *Affection*

A fifth principle of a happy marriage is affection.

A West Germany insurance company made a study and learned that husbands who kiss their wives before leaving for work in the mornings live five years longer than the average male. They also have 20 to 25 percent higher incomes, lose only half as much time through illness, and have fewer accidents.[3]

Affection in marriage is important, not just so that husbands can live longer and have fewer accidents but so that the quality of the marriage can be improved. The kind of affection that is cultivated in constant thought, activated in thoughtful deeds, and expressed in specific ways, is an essential ingredient in a happy marriage.

6. *Adoration*

One last principle is important: adoration. This is the spiritual dimension of the home. A home is not a home without it. One pastor summed it up like this: "Marriage can either be heaven on earth or hell on earth. It will be as much of heaven as there is God in it, and as much hell as there is the devil in it."[4]

Your marriage can be either a little bit of heaven or a whole lot of hell. It depends on you, on whether or not you are willing to adore God so much that you let him be preeminent in your home.

So when you ask, "How can we be parents who honor God?" the first answer is to cultivate the relationship you have with your mate.

Dedication

When you look at the Bible story again, you will discover not only the devotion they had for each other but also the dedication they had to God.

Verse 3 clearly expresses this, "Now this man would go up from his city yearly to worship and to sacrifice to the Lord of hosts in Shiloh" (NASB).

Verse 4 indicates that Elkanah and Hannah were not only regular in their worship attendance but were also faithful in the giving of their resources to God's work.

Their deep dedication to God is also clearly revealed in the prayer of Hannah in verses 11-12.

This is the second important ingredient in the home of Elkanah and Hannah. They had a faith that was deeply felt, genuinely believed, and clearly expressed in the actions of their lives.

Again you may ask, "What does this have to do with parenting?" Again I would answer, "Everything." The quality of the relationship between the parents and God will also inevitably influence the children.

The home can lay a foundation for faith, or it can have a crippling effect. It can be, as Harry Emerson Fosdick once put it, "a hothouse where in a certain isolation of sheltered loyalties beautiful things are grown—affections, sympathies, insights, devotions—which afterwards can be transplanted and applied to the common good of humankind,"[5] or it can stunt growth and inhibit spiritual development.

I'm afraid that we have become somewhat confused at this point. Concerned that we may force our children into a premature decision or an insincere profession of faith, many parents have said, "I'm not going to try to influence my children in matters of religion. When they get old enough, they will just have to decide for themselves." Seeking to be modern and tolerant, we have ended up being irresponsible.

It is true that you cannot force your faith on your child. Neither should you manipulate a child to make a decision before he is ready. But if you fail to provide for the spiritual needs of your child, if you refuse to teach your child about a God of love who has a plan for his life which he revealed in Christ, if you do not provide a spiritual climate in which your child can come to know God, if you fail to develop habits in your child that will make possible a mature spiritual response, then you are avoiding your responsibility as a Christian parent.

A little boy was asked why he loved God. He responded, "I don't know. I guess it just runs in the family." Every child ought to be able to say that about his family.

When Hannah and Elkanah believed in God, and lived out that faith in their lives, then they were taking a second step toward successful parenting.

Determination

Yet another ingredient becomes evident in the story about Hannah and Elkanah: their determination to do everything they could to insure the well-being and proper development of their son.

We see this determination in Hannah when she followed through on the vow she made to God, and in Elkanah as reflected in verse 23. The King James Version translates Elkanah's words to say, "Do what seemeth thee good; tarry until thou have weaned him; only the Lord establish his word." I searched various translations to determine the meaning of that phrase, "The Lord establish his word." *The Living Bible* catches the heart of it with, "May the Lord's will be done."

What did it mean? It meant that Elkanah was willing to do anything so that God's will might be done in relation to their son. Both Hannah and Elkanah were determined to give their very best to their son.

Such determination is the most needed and most often missing ingredient in parenthood today. The favorite word of many parents is *delegation*. We send our children to school to get their education, to the library to get their books, to the park to get their recreation, to the movies for their entertainment, and to the church for their religion. But there are some responsibilities that cannot be delegated. They rest squarely on the shoulders of us parents. If we are to be parents who honor God, then we are going to have to quit delegating all our responsibilities and with a renewed determination dare to develop a quality relationship with our children that will enable us to be the kind of parents God wants us to be.

How can it happen?

1. *We must be available.*

Cross-cultural studies show that US parents spend less time with their children than parents in almost any other country in the world. One study of fathers of middle class families reported that they spend an average of fifteen to twenty minutes a day playing with their one-year-old infants.

In our busy, fast-paced life with its many demands, successful parenting will demand a determination on our part to find quality time to be with our children. Availability is a key ingredient in our relationship with our child.

2. *We must also be approachable.*

At one end of the spectrum is the mother who said, "My daughter tells me everything," and then added, "and I'm a nervous wreck." On the other end are those teenagers who have withdrawn so deeply into what psychologists call "the seclusion syndrome" that there is no family communication at all. Somewhere between those two extremes is where we need to be. It can happen if we have a deep determination to build bridges across the generation gap.

If you will be sensitive to your children's needs, if you will dare to listen in a nonjudgmental way, then you are saying to your child, "Any time you really need me, I'm here. I'm approachable."

3. *We must also be affirming.*

The greatest need your chlid has is to be assured of his personal worth. Every day our children confront forces that call into question their value and worth. Because of that, we parents must be determined to counter the negative, critical, derogatory forces of society with strong doses of affirmation. By what we say, by what we do, by the affection we show to them, by the time we spend with them we need to reassure our children that they are something special. Every child needs to know that he is worth something, not because of what he does, not because of how he acts, not because of his good grades, not because of his accomplishments, but simply because he is a unique individual created and gifted by God. It is our responsibility as parents to communicate that message to our children.

Conclusion

A mother finally put her children to bed, returning to the den for a moment of relaxation only to find a page of the encyclopedia ripped out and torn into little pieces. With tape she carefully pieced the page back together. It was the picture of a child's face. When she finally taped it together she happened to turn it over. There on the other side was a one-page map of the world. And suddenly it struck her—that in putting together the likeness of a child, she had also been giving shape to a world.[7]

That is the overwhelming truth I want to capture your mind. "History is shaped by men, and men are shaped by fathers and mothers." That's why, more than ever before, we need more parents like Hannah and Elkanah who will have the devotion, dedication, and determination to become parents who honor God. Will you?

Notes

1. Richard L. Strauss, *Confident Children and How They Grow* (Wheaton: Tyndale House, 1975), p. 14.

2. Howard J. Clinbell, Jr., *Growth Counseling for Marriage Enrichment* (Philadelphia: Fortress Press, 1975), p. 60.

3. *Quote*, 79:190.

4. Theodore F. Adams, *Making Your Marriage Succeed* (New York: Harper & Brothers, 1953), p. 35.

5. Harry Emerson Fosdick, *The Hope of the World* (New York: Harper & Brothers, 1933), p. 157.

6. John A. Ishee, *From Here to Maturity* (Nashville: Broadman Press, 1975), p. 88.

7. John R. Claypool, "Today's Parenting Challenge," in *Award Winning Sermons* (Nashville: Broadman Press, 1977), 1:20.

5
The Permissive Parent
Eli
1 Samuel 2

I'll never forget the experience. I was sitting with the parents of a fifteen-year-old boy who had shortly before committed suicide. The anguish they felt was indescribable. I could sense by looking into their eyes that something inside them was about to explode. As they tried to talk through their grief that afternoon the same question kept coming up: "Where did we go wrong? We tried to be good parents. We loved our son. But things didn't turn out like we planned. Where did we go wrong?"

That is evidently the question Eli the priest asked himself as he observed the behavior of his sons, Phinehas and Hophni. The Bible calls them sons of Belial (v. 12), which literally means sons of wickedness, hell-raisers! And that's what they were. When the people came to offer their sacrifices to the Lord, Phinehas and Hophni would seize the meat by force and eat it themselves. Verse 17 records that they abhorred the offering of the Lord. Verse 22 reveals that they had sex with the women of the congregation. Verse 24 shows that they were also leading others to have contempt for the offering of the Lord and thus to sin against him. Fine young men, Phinehas and Hophni were!

Phinehas and Hophni were raised in the parsonage, nourished in the Word of God, trained in the work of God, instructed in the worship of God, but the sordid tale told about them in the Bible indicates that they didn't turn out right. The immorality and indifference of his two sons forced Eli to ask the question parents of every generation have asked when their children turn out badly, "Where did we go wrong?"

What does cause children to turn out badly? There is no simple answer to that question.

Some suggest that the key to successful parenting is to expose your children to the church. No one doubts the importance of that. Yet there are many children who are exposed to the church who never catch the faith.

Others suggest that a consistent example is the key. Josh Billings the humorist once said, "Train up a child in the way he should go, and walk there yourself once in a while." True again. Yet some of the finest Christian parents I know are suffering the agony of wayward children.

Still others claim that open communication lines are the key to being successful parents. But there are parents who experience no generation gap with their children who nevertheless have failed to direct their children on a course toward a real life of fulfillment.

Look at our text. Phinehas and Hophni were exposed to the church (the tabernacle). There is every evidence that Eli was a godly man. Verse 23 indicates that the communication lines were open between them.

Yet the two sons of the priest turned out badly. So the questions remains, "How can you explain it when your children turn out badly?" I believe that we are given some insights in our text which will help us answer that question.

Imbalance

When our children turn out badly, the first possible problem is what I call imbalance. If you look at the life of Eli you will discover what we often see in parents today—success in their jobs but failure in their home. That is, there is an imbalance in their lives. They have confused priorities which have led them to put the wrong things first.

Eli was the senior minister at the Shiloh sanctuary, a religious site of significance to Israel. At Shiloh Joshua set up headquarters following the residence at Gilgal (Josh. 14:6; 18:1). It was to Shiloh that many made annual pilgrimages to worship the Lord (Judg. 21:19). It was at Shiloh that the ark of the covenant was kept until the Philistines captured it. The facts that Eli was the priest there and that he carried out his priestly duties well indicate that he was a real success in his ministry.

Perhaps that was the problem. Maybe he was so consecrated to his work, so concerned about doing it well, so consumed with the importance of his position that he did not take time to be with his two sons.

That's what we see in many homes today. The parents, and especially the fathers, are so caught up in the spiral of success that they do not spend much time with their families. There is an imbalance in their lives.

That was David's problem. He was a great man of God. He was a matchless leader. He was an honored king. But he was a poor father. There was an imbalance in his life.

A man I once knew was a success in terms of the world. He was a well-known millionaire. In terms of earthly possessions, he had it all. But his children were insecure and unstable, partly because he had neglected them in his drive for achievement. By the time his grandchildren came along he had extra time, so he tried to make it up to them. On more than one occasion he told me in great sorrow, "I wish I would have spent more time with my children."

That's why so many preachers' children turn out badly—not because they play with the deacons' kids! The reason is that a pastor is so absorbed by the demands of his people, so driven by the desire to please God, so burdened by the hurts which are never completely dealt with that his children are often neglected.

Several years ago, in a missions magazine article, a profile was given of the pastors of the fifteen fastest-growing churches in my denomination. The work habits of one of these leading pastors was described in one word: "Workaholic." About another, these words were used to describe him: "Not a workaholic. He devotes time to family, seeing his number one role as 'being a real spiritual leader in the home.' "[1]

These two contrasting descriptions grabbed my attention. As a self-confessed workaholic I had to look at my own life. The question I found myself asking was this: Which is more important, to be the pastor of one of the fastest-growing churches in the Southern Baptist Convention or to take time to be a father to my children and a husband to my wife? Which is more important, to be a success in the world and have your peers rise up and cheer you or to be a success at home and have your children rise up and call you blessed?

Both are important. But if God has blessed your home with children there is nothing more important for you to do than to train them in the way they should go.

How can we have that time with our children?

1. *Involvement*

That is one of the keys. I've known parents who were overinvolved in their children's lives. But for every one who is overinvolved, there are ten who are underinvolved. Attendance at ball games, playing with the children, late night talks, presence at special events—all of these expressions of involvement communicate to our children that we care.

2. *Individualism*

This is the second key. Susannah Wesley bore nineteen children, some of whom did not survive infancy. In her biography she stated that she gave an hour a week to each child while they were in her home. Uninterrupted, individualized time. After they left home, she spent that same hour a week praying for the child. Hard? You bet it is. Impossible? Not if we are willing to get our priorities straight. We have struggled in our home to give this individualized time. We've not always succeeded. But when we have, we have enjoyed some of our richest parenting experiences.

If you have children, parenthood must be your primary purpose. For when there is an imbalance, when we put success ahead of family, there's a good chance our children will turn out badly.

Indifference

How can you explain it when your children turn out badly? Another possible answer is found in 1 Samuel 3:13. God said of Eli, "His sons made themselves vile, and he restrained them not."

This verse implies an indifference on the part of Eli to properly disciplining his sons. When they needed a firm hand, he simply questioned them about their behavior (2:23). So they just ignored him and went their way. Eli's indifference produced undisciplined children.

Why do parents neglect the matter of discipline?

1. *Commitment*

Sometimes we neglect disciplining our children because we lack commitment. Discipline is hard work and takes time. Many parents are simply not sufficiently committed to the task.

Listen to the commandment of God issued through Moses to the children of Israel: "Hear, O Israel! The Lord is our God, the Lord is one! And you shall love the Lord your God with all your heart and with all your soul and with all your might. And these words, which I am commanding you today, shall be on your heart; and you shall teach them *diligently* to your sons" (Deut. 6:4-7, NASB, author's italics).

With the same diligence with which Satan's power and the world's pressure are working to lead our children in the wrong way, we need to be working to lead our children in the right way.

If we parents do not care enough about our children to

discipline them, we need to rearrange our priorities. If we do not have time to discipline our children, we need to rearrange our schedules.

2. *Confusion*

Sometimes we neglect disciplining our children because of confusion about what discipline involves. James Dobson has said that the greatest social disaster of our century is the idea that love makes discipline unnecessary. Discipline, however, is not the opposite of love. It is the result of love. Discipline which is not for our sake but for the sake of the children, which is not to vent our wrath but to teach our children the comfortable limits in which life is to be lived, is an inescapable outgrowth of love.

Dobson gives this classic suggestion: "When you are defiantly challenged, win decisively. When the child asks 'Who's in charge?' tell him. When he mutters, 'Who loves me?' take him in your arms and surround him with affection."[2] You can mark it down—consistent, firm discipline, given in the context of love, is the key to successful parenthood. But when we like Eli are indifferent to the matter of discipline, seeing the wickedness of our children and restraining them not, then we have a clear explanation of why our children will turn out badly.

Imperfection

How can you explain it when your children turn out badly? There is another hint in the story of Eli, not specifically spelled out in a single verse but implied in the entire narrative. Call it imperfection. That is, sometimes our children turn out badly not because of an imbalance in our lives, not because of an indifference to discipline, but simply because we are human, and as human beings we sometimes make mistakes.

A little boy who brought home his report card with some bad marks on it handed it to his father and said, "Here is my report card. And here is one of your old ones I found in the attic!" He had discovered something we need repeatedly to remind ourselves of: parents are not perfect. They are human beings with human foibles capable of making human errors.

Because of that, you children need to not be so hard on your parents. At times you may think we are dumb. I've got a secret for you. Sometimes we really are. Many times we do not know what is the right thing to do. All we have to guide us are the instincts of our love and the instructions of God's Word which we have to somehow translate into terms of today's world. As a parent I can say there are many times when I want to kick myself for the things I have said and done to my children. Parents are imperfect.

Because of that fact you parents need not be so hard on yourselves. Parenthood is a task for which you have been ill prepared. The more children you have, the more difficult the task becomes. Sometimes when you have done your very best, when you have loved your children with all your heart, when you have disciplined them as best you can, they may still turn out badly because of the human imperfection in your life. In that case you do not need to carry around an unnecessary burden of guilt.

How can we handle our imperfections?

1. *Confront It*

I believe that a fresh breeze would blow across our homes if parents would quit pretending to be perfect and would begin admitting their humanity.

Preachers have the same problem. As a young minister I was in a revival with an older pastor who enjoyed giving advice. I can still remember vividly what he told me as we drove along in his car. "Brian," he counseled, "Don't let the people get close to you because they'll begin to see your weaknesses. And if they know your weaknesses, they'll no longer listen to you." Even at that point in my young ministry, that advice didn't sound right. And it's not right. I've discovered that when people see your humanity as a pastor, when they realize you're in the struggle too, they are ready to listen to the solutions you have discovered in the Word of God.

So it is with parents. Lack of communication is often caused in the home, not because our children see our faults but because we hide our faults. They don't think we're human. So they don't think we would understand.

We are human. We do make mistakes. Let's begin by admitting it.

2. *Confess It*

Have you ever told your child, "I'm sorry I did that; will you forgive me?" Have you ever confessed your humanity to your child?

One night I was in a bad mood. I didn't feel like putting up with anything or anybody. Collin, our second son, kept doing annoying things. (I don't have to explain that, do I, parents?) Finally, I lost my temper, told him he was upsetting everything, and sent him to his room. No sooner had he left the room than I realized it was not he but I who was upsetting everything. I had really blown it. What to do? I decided that I needed to apologize. So I went up to Collin's room, sat down on his bed, and said, "Collin, parents are human, too. Sometimes they make mistakes. That's what I just did. I just blew it, and I'm sorry. Will you forgive me?" He nodded his head and smiled. As I was leaving the room, Collin said, "Dad, if you blow it again, don't worry. I'll forgive you again!"

I'll never forget that night. I hope he doesn't. Because we need to let our children know that we are human.

3. *Communicate About It*

Then, we need to communicate about it. The problem with some of you who are reading this is that your parental errors have been in the distant past. Now your children are gone, and they are living with bitterness and resentment because of your past failures. It's never too late to try to make things right.

On Golden Pond was an unusually moving drama which

dealt primarily with the process of growing old. A minor theme was the relationship between a father and daughter which had many scars on it. Through a grandson the communication lines were opened again between that father and daughter, and a reconciliation was experienced.

That can and should happen to you. And you can make it happen. If you live close to your child, sit down and talk face-to-face. If necessary, make a call or send a note. Not defensively or abusively but humbly and warmly say that you are aware of your mistakes. Confront them. Confess them. Communicate about them. A whole new dimension in your relationship may result.

When our children turn out badly, sometimes it is because of our own imperfections. We did not know enough. We did not love enough. We did not do enough. Deal with it in the three suggestions I have just given. Then, turn it over to the One who is the God of beginning again.

Irresponsibility

How can you explain it when your children turn out badly? There is one more idea here that I want you to see. Call it irresponsibility. I'm not talking about the irresponsibility of Eli now. I'm talking about the irresponsibility of Phinehas and Hophni. When something goes wrong you can't put all the blame on the parents. Each child is a responsible individual, and he is responsible to accept or to reject the heritage his parents provide.

There is a paradox in our text, you see. Samuel, the great prophet of God, was raised in the same home Phinehas and Hophni were raised in. Samuel turned out well; Phinehas and Hophni turned out badly. The difference was not the context of their lives but the commitments of their lives. Samuel built on his godly heritage. Phinehas and Hophni rejected it.

We see the same experience elsewhere in Scripture. Cain

and Abel were raised in the same home. One turned out well and the other turned out badly. Solomon and Absalom were raised in the same household. One turned out well, and the other turned out badly. In each case the difference was not in the parents. It was in the children.

Every child has a chance to choose or reject the heritage of his parents. Ultimately, the reason that Phinehas and Hophni turned out badly was that they refused to build on the heritage their father offered. It was their choice.

Conclusion

Someone said that trying to inculcate Christian principles in our children and raise them properly is like trying to start a fire in the rain. Parenthood is no easy task.

After being careful to balance our lives so that our home takes a place of priority, and after being careful to discipline our children with consistency and love, and after seeking all the help we can to overcome our imperfections, all we can do is just to pray that our children will accept the heritage that we give them, and build on it.

Notes

1. *Home Missions* (December, 1977), pp. 21-25.
2. Dobson, *Dare to Discipline* (Wheaton: Tyndale House, 1970), p. 63.

6
The Pathetic Parent
Samuel
1 Samuel 8:1-3

The story appeared several years ago in *Newsweek* magazine, a story about West German industrialist Friedrich Flick. The article said that when he died,

> He left a personal fortune estimated at 1.5 billion dollars, a business empire that embraced all or part of some 300 firms and a reputation as perhaps the crustiest, craftiest magnate ever to operate on the German business scene. . . . Unlike such German industrialists as Alfred Krupp, Robert Bosch, and Ernst von Siemens, he never really made anything; he simply put companies together. "He always made the right moves," summed up one awed observer. "He was the Bobby Fischer of the industrialist world."
>
> At his death, the Flick empire generated annual sales in excess of $3 billion. But for all his enormous power and wealth, *the old man had one very human shortcoming: he could not control his family.* By last week a Flick family fight over *der alter Herr's* empire had employees, bankers and politicians alike shuddering over the eventual impact it might have on the West German economy.[1]

This news report tells us that Friedrich Flick could put companies together. He could alter the economy of a nation. He could make money. But his one "*very human shortcoming*" was that he could not control his family.

This story rang a responsive chord in my mind when I read about the family of Samuel. Samuel was one of the preeminent personalities of the Old Testament. He could lead Israel to conquer the Philistines. He could administer a nation. He could represent God. But he had one very human shortcoming—he could not control his family. While Samuel succeeded in so many areas of his life the text makes it clear that he failed as a father.

In what ways did he fail?

Failed to Learn from Experience

The first thing we see is that Samuel failed to learn from experience.

Remember the home in which Samuel was reared. He was the son of Elkanah and Hannah. Because his mother had dedicated him to the Lord, Samuel went to live with Eli, the priest, and it was in his home that Samuel grew up.

What did he see? He saw a father who was a successful priest at the Shiloh sanctuary but who neglected his role as a father. Eli did not discipline his sons. He did not instruct his sons. He did not guide his sons. He did not spend time with his sons. The result was that the Bible says, "The sons of Eli were worthless men" (1 Sam. 2:12, RSV). We just discussed that tragic story in the last chapter. Samuel saw firsthand the result when a father neglects his responsibility as a parent. Experience told him that parenthood had to be given priority, that children had to be loved, disciplined, and guided. But notice that Samuel ended up doing the same thing Eli had done. He failed to learn from experience.

Someone has suggested that experience is what enables you to recognize a mistake when you make it again. That's what experience was for Samuel. Rather than being a lesson that motivated him to do differently, it was a model which he imitated.

Recent studies indicate the same thing happening in families today.

The National Institute on Alcohol Abuse and Alcoholism has

conducted extensive research revealing that children of alcoholics suffer a high risk of developing alcoholism themselves in
later years. Instead of being motivated never to drink by their
unhappy experiences with alcoholic parents, these children are
twice as likely to become alcoholics as other children.[2]

A study on family violence written by Murray Straus and
Richard Gelles indicated that abused children are more likely
to become abusing parents. Rather than being motivated
never to use physical violence because of the unhappy experiences with abusive parents, when these children grow up they
become abusers themselves at a rate four times greater than
adults whose parents did not beat them.[3]

The model of the home in which we grow up largely
determines the husband/father or wife/mother that we will
become. We see this patently portrayed in the Scriptures.
Abraham lied about his relationship with his wife to avoid
danger (Gen. 12:11-19). Later, Abraham's son Isaac did the
same thing (Gen. 26:7-10). Jacob lied to his father to conceal
his deception (Gen. 27:18-24). Later, Jacob's sons lied to him
in the same way (Gen. 37:31-34). David took Bathsheba
because he desired her, ignoring the feelings and rights of
others (2 Sam. 11:1-4). Later, David's son Amnon did the same
thing to Tamar (2 Sam. 13:1-14).

Most often one's childhood home is not an experience that
motivates a person to do differently but a model which one will
eventually follow oneself. So it was for Samuel. Experience
should have taught him the priority of parenting, the folly of
fathers who neglect their sons, the incompleteness of life when
success at work is not matched by success at home. Experience
should have taught Samuel these lessons, but Samuel failed to
learn from experience.

This is a message for fathers and mothers of today.

What you do in your home, how you relate to each other as
husband and wife, how you express your love to your children,
how you spend your time, how consistent you are in your

discipline, how genuine you are in your religious faith, how you relate to money, how you handle emergencies, how you react to tragedy—all of these matters are so vitally important because they will provide the primary model for your children when, later on, they form their own families.

You can perpetuate a pattern of neglect which leads to heartbreak, as Eli did, or you can carry on a pattern of concern that leads to fulfillment. It is true that children do learn what they live. What you do wrong in your home will likely be continued in the homes of your children.

There is also a message here for fathers and mothers of the future, for young people reading this who some day will be parents.

You need to understand that your parents are human. They make mistakes. Some things they do right; others they do wrong. Consequently, the model of parenting and family life which they provide for you is not perfect.

Now you can't change the way your parents are. As one child wrote in an essay on parents, "We get our parents at such a late age it is impossible to change their habits." Your responsibility is not to change your parents but to take the bad they give you and improve on it. Then, take the good they give you and build on it. That is, learn from their mistakes as well as their successes. You can be a successful parent if you will blend the experiences of life with the expressions of God's Word to develop the proper model for your home.

Failed to Develop His Children

There is a second failure of Samuel apparent in the text. He failed to develop his children at the proper rate.

Sometimes this is reflected in our tendency to develop our children too slowly by overprotecting them. One of the most difficult ideas to accept as parents is that we are preparing our children to leave us. Eventually our children are going to leave us and will have to face the world with the tools that we have given them. We are equipping them for life, so when the time comes they will be able to make it on their own.

We need to prepare them *intellectually* by exposing them to ideas and thoughts, books and magazines that will turn on their creative potential.

We need to prepare them *spiritually* by giving them a faith to stand on and then helping them as they struggle to make that faith their own. Timothy Dwight, an early president of Yale University, once said that he wanted his children exposed to teachings of atheism while he was still around to refute them.[4]

We need to prepare them *emotionally* for the realities of life's problems. I heard this little poem the other day:

> The world will never adjust itself
> To suit your whims to the letter.
> Some things will go wrong
> Your whole life long
> And the sooner you know it the better. (Author unknown)

That's a lesson we need to teach our children. Overindulged children whose every desire is fulfilled will become maladjusted adults.

We need to prepare our children for *decision making* by providing opportunities to make decisions in as many areas as they can. Confidence is developed as they see the results of decisions they have made for themselves.

The admonition to "train up a child in the way he should go" (Prov. 22:6) is a challenge to every parent to avoid the kind of overprotection that will fail to develop our children at a rapid enough rate to face the exigencies that they face each day and that they will someday face.

Charles Swindoll, in his book *You and Your Child,* suggests five things that every father should teach his son.[5] I believe they apply equally well to daughters.

1. *Confidence*
We should teach our children how to stand alone in the

world. This happens when they are aware of their own self-worth and when they have a confident faith. When an individual knows who he is and whose he is, he will have the inner strength to stand firm against the pressures of the world.

2. *Correction*

We also need to teach our children that correction is a part of life and that they should therefore respect those in authority over them. A sensitivity to instruction and a respect for authority are invaluable birthrights to give to our children.

3. *Courage*

Our young people will be constantly confronted by temptation. We need to help them to know how to deal with it. Temptation is of course no new phenomenon in the human race. The magnitude of it in our day, however, is frightening.

A mother and her daughter were watching a late, late movie together one night. This was one of those golden oldies which dated back to the mother's childhood. The movie was a typical romantic movie which ended with the hero and his girl on the verge of a kiss. As they moved closer together, the music came to a crescendo, the lights faded out, and the movie was over. The mother asked her daughter, "What do you think of the way movies used to be?" The daughter replied, "Gee, mom, your movies ended where ours begin!" That's an accurate assessment of the times. Temptation confronts our children with greater pressure than ever. Consequently, we need to help our children be prepared for temptation by: warning them about it; reminding them of the consequences of evil; helping them develop a healthy attitude toward sex; and helping them to learn the wisdom of the Scriptures.

4. *Cash*

We need also to teach our children about money—how to earn it, how to spend it, how to give it, and how to save it. We need to teach them the value of money by providing opportunities for them to earn it. We need to teach them how to use money with an allowance.

There is more to life than money. But the use of money is a key matter that determines every other aspect of our lives. Therefore, we need to train our children.

5. *Contribution*

We also need to teach our children that the best way they can make a contribution to life is to learn how to work. I have discussed the Christian principles of work in my book, *Famous Singles of the Bible.*[6] Let me simply say here that we need to teach our children these basic principles concerning work: to work hard and happily; to think while they work; to learn how to cooperate with others; and to finish the job. In this way, they can make a significant contribution to life.

There is another side to the coin, however. While some parents hinder the proper development of their children by overprotection, others rush the development of their children by exposing them to things for which they are not yet ready.

This was Samuel's problem. He knew his sons, their abilities, their attitudes, their allegiances in life. He knew that they were not ready to be exalted to the position of judge over Israel, but he forced them into it anyway. The result was disastrous for them and for Israel.

I know parents who seem bent on eliminating childhood. They push their children into situations before they can handle them. They confront them with decisions they are not yet able to make, exposing them to ideas they are not mature enough to deal with, giving them responsibilities they are not able to handle. The result is not development but disaster.

Instead of allowing the lives of their children to bloom at the proper rate under the patient nourishment of loving concern, they force them to blossom before they are ready.

Someone has suggested that the role of a parent is that of a doorkeeper. We would not allow a stranger to come through our door to harm our children. In the same way we should not allow ideas, experiences, responsibilities, and decisions that our children are not ready for to come through the door to harm them. A family is a door with hinges and a lock. We must open the door and close the door at the right time.[7]

Sometimes by overprotecting our children and at other times by pushing our children, we fail to help them develop at the proper rate to face the challenges at each stage of their lives. That was the failure of Samuel.

Conclusion

Parenthood is life's greatest responsibility. What a shame it would be to have this commentary given of our lives: they made money, visited places, held offices of importance in the community, but they had one "very human shortcoming," they could not control their families. What a tragedy!

Notes

1. *Newsweek,* Sept. 25, 1972. Used by permission.
2. *Quote,* 71:723.
3. *Quote,* 79:344.
4. Clyde E. Fant, Jr., and William M. Pinson, Jr., eds., *Twenty Centuries of Great Preaching* (Waco: Word Books, 1971), 3:177.
5. Charles R. Swindoll, *You & Your Child* (New York: Bantam Books, 1980), pp. 102-116.
6. See pp. 23-27 of the book referred to.
7. Edith Schaeffer, *What Is a Family?* (Old Tappan: Fleming H. Revell Co., 1975), pp. 211 ff.

7
The Prominent Parent
David
2 Samuel 18—19

Paul Harvey wrote about his son, "My son, my son . . . has given me a gift more precious than any. He has given up his identity for me." Discussing the problems of the children of prominent people, Paul Harvey explained that "it is not so much a matter of 'neglect' as the fact that the children of the famous are never, themselves, anybody." Sons and daughters of the famous have as their privilege "ever to be a pronoun, never to be a noun."[1]

Could that have been the reason that David of biblical history knew such tragic experiences with his children? David's sin with Bathsheba certainly affected the lives of his children. On that the Bible is clear. But could it not also be true that much of the trouble David's children experienced came simply because they were *David's* children?

Of the great men of Israel's history, David was preeminent. He was a man after God's heart, the sweet psalmist of Israel, the mighty deliverer of his people, the model of the messianic expectations of the Jews. David was a magnificent monarch, a fearless warrior, and a gifted musician. He was the most famous man in Israel in his day.

David was also a father. In the unfolding story of David's life as king of Israel, we also see the development of his life as a father. Clearly portrayed in the experience of David are the trials and triumphs of parenthood.

The Trials

No one sees more clearly, firsthand, the trials of parenthood than does a pastor. More times than I like to admit I have sat with and cried with parents over their children. Gone is the joy with which the parents welcomed that child into their home. Crushed almost beyond recovery is the pride those parents felt in the early progress of that child. The trials and tragedies of parenthood have rushed full force into their lives.

At times the trials are of a temporary and trivial nature. Such was the case of one set of parents who placed this advertisement in the paper: "For sale, complete collection of rock and roll records, cheap price. If a boy answers, hang up and call back later."

More often, the trials reach the more serious level expressed in this poem:

> My flower child has gone to seed—
> has gone to pot—
> Is smoking weed
> He whispers peace but what it means
> Is sitting sadly in his jeans.
> He mentions love more fervently—
> Yet all the love must come from me.[2]

David did not have to face the dilemma of drugs. Yet he certainly knew the trials of parenthood. Illustrated in his family are several of the primary trials of parenthood.

1. Rebellion

Read the story of David's family, and you will discover that he knew the trials of rebellion. Ken Chafin tells of a retired military man who felt that the best way to operate a family was on the military system. His children were awakened by reveille. Before breakfast each day, they had to line up for inspection. After the father had issued the "orders for the day" on one occasion, he asked, "Are there any questions?" His youngest son replied, "Yes, how does one transfer out of this chicken outfit?"[3]

David's son Absalom wanted to transfer out of the chicken outfit he was in. The story of how it happened is told in 2 Samuel 13—18. This rebellious spirit originated in the crisis caused by the death of Amnon. The rebellious spirit was increased when David refused to see Absalom. Absalom, bitter toward his father, not only rebelled against David but also turned the people of Israel against David. As the biblical writer expressed it in 2 Samuel 15:6 (NASB), "And in this manner Absalom dealt with all Israel who came to the king for judgment; so Absalom stole away the hearts of the men of Israel." Finally, this rebellious spirit erupted into open conspiracy as Absalom stole the throne from David, and David had to flee for his life.

Perhaps the greatest tragedy of parenthood is to have a child turn his heart against you in open rebellion. Yet, it happens. During 1975, over 260,000 youngsters under seventeen years of age ran away for at least a week. On dozens of occasions I have sat with parents who have shared with me the heartbreaking news of children who have run away from home.

Where does this rebellion come from? Often, rebellion grows out of complaints the children have toward their parents for which they never find a satisfactory solution. Gary Collins has listed several common complaints that children have about their parents. Among these complaints are the following: Parents do not recognize that teenagers are human beings with needs and feelings; parents fail to observe the elementary rules of courtesy toward their teenagers; parents are contemptuous of teenagers' property rights; parents meddle too much; parents expect too much; parents do not allow teenagers their privacy, and parents do not consider the effect on their children when they make major decisions.[4] When these problems continue without ever being addressed or dealt with, rebellion is often the result.

Sometimes our criticism of our children is justified, based on their behavior. Such constructive criticism is a part of our parental responsibility. Problems arise, however, when we create a negative atmosphere in which we are always critical.

Dr. Frederick Flach of Cornell University Medical College talks about a "depressogenic environment" which prevails in many homes. He defines this environment as "one that provides no ego support, prevents one from becoming self-reliant, repeatedly stirs up hostility, and at the same time blocks its release, provokes unnecessary guilt, or causes one to feel lonely and rejected."[5] Parents who maintain this "depressogenic environment" are creating the atmosphere in which rebellion finds root.

What is the solution? No simple answers will do at this point. Yet, three steps are basic to any solution. First, keep the lines of communication open. The second step is to seek to determine the source of the problem. The third step is to take constructive measures to deal with the problem.

David's role model at this point is instructive only in that he shows us what *not* to do. Instead of opening the communication lines with his son, David closed them. Second Samuel 14:24 says that David told Joab about Absalom: " 'Let him turn to his own house, and let him not see my face.' So Absalom turned to his own house and did not see the king's face" (NASB). When David refused to communicate with his son, he made it impossible to solve the problem. Consequently, this rebellious spirit resulted in open rebellion toward David,.

To give birth to a child, watch him grow, provide for his needs, and then to see that child rebel against you—that is one of the trials of parenthood.

2. *Rivalry*

Study the tale of David's family, and you will discover that he also knew the trials of rivalry among his children.

A Sunday School teacher asked her class of boys if any of the Ten Commandments spoke to us about our relationship with our parents. "Yes," responded one little boy, "One of the Commandments says, 'Honour thy father and thy mother.'" "That was good," the teacher said. "Does one of the Ten Commandments have to do with the relationship between brothers?" "Yes," replied another youngster. "Which Commandment is that?" queried the teacher. The youngster added, "Thou shalt not kill."

Nonparents or people without siblings might not understand that youngster's response. Parents of two or more children certainly will. I often feel more like a referee than a parent. From morning until night sibling rivalry fluctuates between cold war and open conflict.

David's household was also disturbed by sibling rivalry. The experience of Tamar, Absalom, and Amnon in 2 Samuel 13 is a clear example. Amnon's desire for his half sister, Tamar, led him to rape her. To avenge the disgrace Amnon caused Tamar, Absalom killed him.

Sibling rivalry appears again in the political maneuvering near the end of David's life. First Kings 1 tells the intriguing story of Adonijah and Solomon, two sons of David who desired the throne. When the dust settled Solomon was king, and Adonijah was dead (2:24-25).

Why do brothers and sisters see themselves as rivals? Why do they fight so much?

Rudolf Dreikurs has suggested four motivations for the actions of our children. "Attention" is the first motivation. If the child does not feel loved, he will misbehave to draw attention to himself. "Power" is a second motivation. If the child does not feel that he has achieved, he will misbehave to show that he has too much power for others to stop him. "Revenge" is a third motivation. If the child is afraid others will reject or hurt him, he will strike out to keep them from hurting him. The fourth motivation is "inadequacy." If a child does not feel adequate, he will misbehave to prove that he is indeed inadequate.[6] Conflicts between siblings often grow out of these four motivations.

What is the solution? Part of the solution is to accept sibling rivalry as an inescapable trial of parenthood. A certain amount of it is inevitable. Three steps are basic to solving the problem of excessive sibling rivalry. First, help each child to feel important. Individual attention and affirmation is important at this point. Second, help each child to feel that he belongs. Affection and articulating that affection are important at this point. Third, help each child to achieve. Find something the child can do well and encourage him in this area.

To have the harmony of the home disrupted with sibling rivalry—that is another of the trials of parenthood.

3. *Repercussions*

A third trial of parenthood is clearly evident in the story of David: the repercussions of our actions in the lives of our children. Each individual is ultimately responsible for his own life. Nevertheless, impact on our lives by significant others, especially parents, strongly influences us.

Second Samuel 11 records David's double sin of adultery with Bathsheba and the murder of her husband. The immediate repercussion of David's heinous sin was the death of the child conceived in his act of infamy with Bathsheba (2 Sam. 12:14). The long-term repercussions were expressed by the prophet Nathan in 2 Samuel 12:9-12 (NASB):

" 'Why have you despised the word of the Lord by doing evil in His sight? You have struck down Uriah the Hittite with the sword, have taken his wife to be your wife, and have killed him with the sword of the sons of Ammon. Now therefore, the sword shall never depart from your house, because you have despised Me and have taken the wife of Uriah the Hittite to be your wife.' Thus says the Lord, 'Behold, I will raise up evil against you from your own household; I will even take your wives before your eyes, and give them to your companion, and

he shall lie with your wives in broad daylight. Indeed you did it
secretly, but I will do this thing before all Israel, and under the
sun.' "

More tragic than what our children do for us through their
rebellion and rivalry is *what we do to them*. Our self-
centeredness often deprives them of proper opportunities for
self-development. Our lack of affection robs them of the
emotional support they need for proper growth. Our bad
habits become negative patterns which strongly tempt them to
duplicate these same patterns in their lives. Our prejudices
often become their prejudices. We sin, and the repercussions
of our sins affect the lives of our children in ways too numerous
to mention. That is one of the greatest trials of parenthood.

What is the solution? The first step is recognition. Not only
do we have to reap what we sow, but in many ways and on
many occasions, our children also have to reap what we sow.
We need to recognize the impact we make on the lives of our
children. The second step is recommitment. The best way to
save our children from having to reap the ill fruit of our
undisciplined lives is to redirect our energies to living disciplined, holy lives.

Triumphs

There is another side to the coin of parenthood, a positive
side. As a parent, we not only experience trials. We also enjoy
triumphs. We not only encounter tragedies. We also experience thrills. The Bible tells us that David knew the triumphs of
parenthood.

1. *Growth*
One of the greatest triumphs of a parent is to watch the
growth of a child as he develops toward adulthood. David
knew that joy. Mixed in with the tragedies of children who
destroyed their lives was the development of Solomon into a

wise, mature, talented leader of Israel. The joy this brought to David as a parent more than compensated for the heartaches that he had to endure.

When our fourth child was born, our oldest child was only six years old. Trying to handle four babies was no easy task for my wife. Older mothers would often tell her, "These are the best years of your life. Parenthood becomes a greater burden as the children grow up." Contrary to that prophecy, we have discovered that as the children have grown and matured, our joy has multiplied. Why? Because sharing in the growth of our children is one of the triumphant blessings of parenthood.

2. *Guidance*

Another triumphant joy of parenthood is to see the guidance of God in the lives of our children.

Several years ago it was my distinct privilege to meet Mrs. Summers whose son, Dr. Ray Summers, is one of the most respected New Testament scholars of our generation. This dear saint, nearly ninety years of age, delighted in talking about her "boy." Her eyes twinkled, and her heart was overjoyed as she talked about what her son had accomplished. Why such joy? Because her son's life had been touched by God's Spirit to the extent that all of his life had been lived under the guidance of God.

3. *Goals*

Another triumphant joy of parenthood is to see our children reach their goals in life and know that we had a part in it.

This was why David's heart was broken when he learned that his son Absalom had been killed. Absalom would never be able to reach the goals which were compatible with his potential (2 Sam. 18:33).

In contrast, what a joy it is to see a child grow toward maturity, respond to the guidance of God in his life, and reach the goals which he has set.

Care must be exercised to recognize and accept the unique

individuality of each child. Success is not to be measured by what our children accomplish but by how their accomplishments match their potential.

A friend said to Harry Truman's mother, "You must be proud of your son in the White House." "Yes, I am," Mrs. Truman responded. "And I have a son down the street I'm proud of too."[7]

Parental pride and incomparable joy come when our children reach the significant goals they have set for their lives. That is one of the triumphant blessings of parenthood.

Conclusion

A forty-year-old man was the most eligible bachelor in a North Georgia community. He left his hometown to seek his fortune. Several months later he returned home to share some exciting news with his father. "Pop," exclaimed the man, "I just got married." "Well, Son," replied the father, "that's good." "But she sure is ugly," continued the son. "Well," returned the father, "that's bad." "But," added the newly married man, "she is really rich." "Well," answered the father, "that's good." "But," the son explained, "she sure is stingy." "Well," said the father, "that's bad." "But," the boy continued, "she did build a new house for me." "Well," replied the father, "that's good." "But," the son added, "the house just burned down." "Well," answered the father, "that sure is bad." When the son added, "And she was in it!" the father did not know what to say.

Is parenting good or bad? It is *good* and *bad*. Both trials and triumphs come to parents of every age.

Notes

1. *Quote,* 92:221.
2. *Proclaim,* April, 1977, p. 12.

3. Kenneth Chafin, *Is There a Family in the House?* (Waco: Word Books, 1978), p. 90.

4. Gary R. Collins, *Man in Transition* (Carol Stream, Illinois: Creation House, 1971), p. 76.

5. Alice Kosner, "What to Do When You're Really Depressed," *McCalls,* November, 1977, p. 282.

6. Quoted in Don H. Highlander, *Positive Parenting* (Waco: Word Books, 1980), p. 123.

7. James Hightower, ed., *Illustrating the Gospel of Matthew* (Nashville: Broadman Press, 1982), p. 16.

8
The Peerless Parent
Mary
Luke 1:39-56

Who can make a model of a mother? She must be tender and yet tough, reasonable and yet romantic, assertive and yet affectionate. Who can make a model of a mother? I believe the closest we have to a model for motherhood in the New Testament is Mary, the mother of our Lord.

Several cameo shots are given of Mary in the New Testament. In Luke 1, we view her reaction to the announcement of Jesus' birth. In Luke 2, we see her response when Jesus remained in the Temple to converse with the scholars when she and Joseph started back to Nazareth. In John 2, we read about Mary's request for help from her son at a wedding. In Matthew 12 (and parallels), we see Mary seeking Jesus as he wanders through Galilee preaching, in an attempt to persuade him to come home. In John 19, we behold her standing in the shadow of the cross as her son dies like the common criminal his contemporaries declared him to be. In Acts 1:14, we find Mary as a believer, dwelling with the disciples in Jerusalem.

In these few brief glimpses, we are given a revealing picture of our Lord's mother. The great need of our day is for principles which will enable us to be more effective parents. In the Bible, we discover a surprising lack of such principles on how to be a good mother or a good father. Instead, we find various models from which we can glean principles that were hammered out in the crucible of human experience. Mary is one of those models. Several principles emerge from the model of Mary.

Amenable

Perhaps the first truth we see about Mary is that she was amenable to God. Perhaps the most important insight into her character is seen in Luke 1:38. After the angel had announced to Mary what would happen, this was her response: "I am the Lord's servant, and I am willing to do whatever he wants" (TLB).

Mary laid the groundwork for a successful relationship with her son by settling her relationship with God. She gave top priority to spiritual matters. She was yielded to God in her own life. Therefore, she could create a spiritual environment in her home that would enable her son to grow into the man God created him to be.

The greatest hindrance to successful parenthood today is not lack of knowledge but lack of commitment. It is not that we don't know what to do. The problem is that we are not willing to do it. Instead of saying with Mary, "I am the Lord's servant, and I am willing to do whatever he wants," we say, "I am in charge here, and I will do what I want," or "I am liberated, and I need to fulfill myself," or "I have needs, too, and I'll meet them first."

Do you want to be a good parent? Do you want to reach a time in your life when your children rise up and call you blessed? This is the first principle: be amenable to the demands of God. Like Mary, be willing to say, "I am the Lord's servant, and I am willing to do whatever he wants."

A pivotal question arises at this point. How do you discover God's direction? How do you know what God wants you to do? Prayer is the key. Prayer is not just a series of petitions that we direct heavenward. Instead, prayer is primarily tuning in to God, locking in on his wavelength. Proper parenting develops most readily from the fertile soil of daily devotion to God.

A basic biblical model for prayer is found in James 5:16: "The effective prayer of a righteous man can accomplish much." Three principles for prayer are described in that verse.

1. A Righteous Life

It is the prayer of a righteous man, James states, that accomplishes much (5:16). James is not saying that only an especially righteous person can pray. Prayer is a privilege of every Christian. But James is saying that there is a correlation between the condition of our lives and the effect of our prayers. Any Christian can talk to God. But effective prayers grow out of the lives of a righteous person.

2. A Passionate Concern

The word *effective* comes from the Greek word which is the root word from which "energy" comes. A better English equivalent of the Greek word is "energetic." It is prayer, as one commentator puts it, in which the worshiper is possessed. Effective prayers are those uttered with such passion, with such energy, with such fervency, with such an overwhelming sense of need that you are literally possessed by your experience of prayer.

3. A Persistent Practice

James indicates that effective prayer is also persistent prayer. The word translated "effective" also carries with it the idea of persistence. It speaks of the kind of prayer that cannot be denied. This persistent quality of prayer becomes clearer in the example James used in verses 17-18 to illustrate his point. Referring to the experiences of Elijah in 1 Kings 17:1 to 18:41-46, James illustrates the kind of prayer that issues in results, the persistent kind of prayer that will not give up until the answer comes.

Commitment to God is the first principle in effective parenthood. True commitment to God will lead to and feed on a daily life of prayer.

Attentive

We also note that Mary was attentive to the needs of her son.

After the visit of the shepherds to see the baby Jesus, Luke made this statement about Mary, "But Mary treasured up all these things, pondering them in her heart" (Luke 2:19, NASB). To ponder means to cast back and forth in the mind, to put the facts down side by side for the purpose of comparison.

After the experience with Jesus in the Temple, the Bible says, "His mother treasured all these things in her heart" (Luke 2:51, NASB). The word *treasure* means to keep thoroughly. She kept going over and over these things in her mind.

Mary not only was attuned to the purpose of God, but she was also in tune with happenings in the life of her son. She gave careful consideration to what he thought, what he said, how he felt, and what he needed. She was tuned in to her son. She knew him.

I wonder, how well do you know your children? Do you know their friends? Do you know what they really enjoy doing? Do you know what kind of music they listen to? Do you know what they are reading? Do you know what their dreams are? Do you know the problems they are going through? How well do you know your children? How attuned are you to what they are doing? How attentive are you to their needs? How much time do you spend pondering in your heart those matters which relate to your children?

One father told his daughter as she left for a date that he wanted her to be in by midnight. She protested, "But, Daddy, this is such a special night. It is the school prom. And besides," she added, "I'm not a child anymore." The father put down his paper, looked at his daughter, and said, "You're right. You're not a child any more. You'd better be in by eleven!" He had been so busy he had not noticed his daughter was growing up.

How long has it been since you took a close look at those children? How long since you listened to them with full attention? There are times during every week when your children need you to be available to them emotionally and physically. If you're not, they will interpret that inattention and inaccessibility as rejection. And it could have serious repercussions in their lives.

A graduate student working on juvenile delinquency reported back to his sociology seminar that he was having difficulties collecting data. His plan was to call a dozen homes at about 9:00 PM to ask the parents if they knew where their children were at that hour. "My first five calls," he complained, "were answered by children who had no idea where their parents were!"[1]

Juvenile delinquency often begins with parental delinquency. Parents, when your children need you the most, do they know where you are?

Do you want to be a good parent? Do you want to reach a time in your life when your children rise up and call you blessed? Then let them know you are available to them, whenever and however they need you. Make them aware that you are sensitive to their needs, that you are attentive to their feelings. Like Mary, be willing to treasure all these things and ponder them in your heart.

Again, a pivotal question emerges. How do you discern the dreams and desires of your child? How do you know what he wants to do? Time is the key. To know your child you must spend time with him. But how can you find enough time? Several principles will help.

1. *Set Priorities*

This is the first step. Put a high priority on time with your children. You will never have time with your children unless you decide that you need to, that it is important. In his recent book *The Caring Father,* Dr. Wilson Wayne Grant uses an event from his own life to emphasize the importance of spending quality time with their children.

> My schedule was crushing me. I could see I wouldn't be on time for dinner so I hastily called home. Kristen, then eight years old, answered.
> "Honey, I'm going to be late," I said.
> "Well, Dad," she interrupted, "come home soon. I've got something to show you."

Kristen had a personal interest in her daddy coming home. She wanted to show me her report card because she was happy and proud of her four A's. She wanted to share her joy and excitement with me. In another way, though, she was speaking for children all over America. "Daddy, come home!" they are calling to their fathers. It is the fortunate child whose father is tuned in enough to receive this message and come home. As we will see, children of all ages need their fathers very much. They yearn to share—they need to share—their joys and hurts, their hopes and dreams with a father who can be seen, felt, and heard. They crave a father who listens, touches, and cares.

Not long afterward, I was on my way to the study, coffee cup in hand, ready to do more work. *I'm really getting into my subject,* I thought, and was in a hurry to begin.

As I whipped around the doorway in the hall, Kristen blocked my way, holding a big picture puzzle with both hands.

"Dad, will you help me with my puzzle?" she asked almost timidly.

I was caught in a dilemma—a dilemma I think often confronts fathers today. I honestly enjoy working puzzles with Kristen. But at the moment, my thoughts were focused on the job at hand. The conflict between responsibility to family and loyalty to job is the either-or choice that we fathers often seem to face.

What should I do?

I chose to spend a few minutes helping Kristen with her puzzle. When we were finished, I ran to the typewriter. Kris was happy with the puzzle and the few minutes I had given to her. My progress in the study was not seriously impeded. And coming out of this experience I had a clear conscience. . . .

In such situations, I used to think, *I just don't have time to be the kind of father I want to be.* But I'm discovering I can make time for those things that truly count. And I've come to see that being an effective father is near the top of the list of things that finally count in a man's life. It's not easy, but when I try I've found it possible to give proper attention to my family while being loyal to my profession and my responsibility to earn a living. Our society seems to say, "If things can be standardized and mass-produced, why not children?" If we give them the best medical care, the best food, the best kindergarten, and the best school, then they are bound to come out OK. But we know this isn't so. For if they do not receive the proper kind of attention from us, all these other things are so much whistling in the wind.[2]

2. *Plan*

The second step is to plan time. Recognizing that it is essential to have the time, this time must be planned. It will not just happen. Plan this time around the activities of the children. Being at ball games, award ceremonies for the organizations in which the children are involved, or watching them perform will help communicate to your children that you care. Plan special meals with each of the children. Plan times for the entire family to be together in fun times. Plan.

3. *Protect*

Once the plans have been made, protect those times from all the enemies that would steal these precious moments from you. Learning to say no to lesser important demands so that we can give attention to a high priority demand, time spent with children, is a difficult but necessary lesson to learn for parents in today's world.

Knowledge of your child is the second principle of effective parenthood. This knowledge grows out of quality time spent with that child.

Aspiring

There is a third principle here: Mary was also aspiring. We see this in the presentation of Jesus in the Temple when he was eight days old. We see this in the pattern of religious commitment that is implied in the visit to the Temple when Jesus was twelve. Mary was not only devoted to God and sensitive to her son. She was also willing to create the proper spiritual environment in which her son could develop. She had goals before her son, high ideals of character and commitment that helped mold him into the special instrument of God.

I have seen successful people who did not have that kind of environment in which to grow up. I have seen Christian young people come out of homes in which God's name was never uttered, except in an oath. But I have seen so many more in whose lives the seeds of faith were planted by committed parents. I've seen more who had those seeds nourished and cultivated by loving Christian parents until they themselves bloomed into devoted servants of Christ.

Do you want to be a good parent? Then create within your home a strong spiritual environment in which your children can grow spiritually. Don't be afraid that you will force your faith on your children. More fatal is the attitude of parents who give their children no faith at all. Don't be afraid that you will make your child decide for God. More fatal is the action of parents who live in such a way that their children never have an opportunity to decide for God. Like Mary, be willing to create a spiritual environment with high ideals toward which your children can reach. Be an aspiring parent.

What about goal setting for our children's lives? How can we help our children set goals for their lives? Several principles will help.

1. *Personal*

The goals for our children should be personal. That is, these goals should be their goals, not ours. We can provide the wisdom of our experience. We can tell our children what certain goals will demand of them. We can be resource persons. But for the goals to be realistic, they have to be personal.

2. *Potential*

Then, these goals must relate to the potential of the child. The Bible speaks on this matter in 1 Corinthians 12. Each Christian is given a gift by the Holy Spirit. These gifts are given for the purpose of carrying out certain ministries. Thus, the goals that we set for our lives should be related to these gifts and in line with these ministries.

3. *Pliable*

Goals must be pliable. Life is so complex that it is impossible to chart out a lifetime from the perspective of the present. As never before, we need to be flexible in our personal planning. We must help our children to realize that as circumstances change in life, our goals will often need to change. A pliability in goal setting will allow for these changes.

To help our children set reachable goals which challenge them to their maximum output is the third principle of effective parenting. Such goals emerge out of the God-given gifts in their lives.

Affectionate

One more principle emerges in the story of Mary. She was amenable, attentive, aspiring, and she was affectionate.

In Japan, there is a mountainous area which for centuries has been called, "The Place Where You Leave Your Mother." It was so named because of the custom of taking the old and feeble up to the top of the mountain to die. One day a strong young man carried his aged mother through the dense forest. As they moved up the mountain for the purpose both understood but neither talked about, the young man began to notice something. "Why," he asked his mother, "do you continue to break small branches along the way?" Looking at him through eyes dimmed by everything but love, she said, "So that you will not get lost on the way back home."

Mary had that kind of love for her son. Even when he chided her for her lack of understanding in the Temple, even when he rebuked her when she called for his assistance at the wedding in Cana, even when he refused to go with her when she sought to take him away, even when he was hung on the criminal's cross, even then Mary still loved him. Hers was a love that would not let him go.

Do your children realize your love for them is so deep they can never do anything to destroy it? Do your children understand that regardless of what they do, how far they stray, or how deep they fall, you will always be there to forgive, welcome them back home, and help them pick up the pieces of their lives? Do your children sense that you really care? Have you told them lately? Have you shown them?

Virginia Satir says that it takes four hugs a day for survival, eight hugs for maintenance, and twelve for growth.[3] Have you hugged your children today? A key ingredient of successful parenthood is love that grows and shows.

Conclusion

An old Jewish saying teaches us: "God couldn't be everywhere, so he created mothers." Mothers who follow the pattern of Mary, who dare to be amenable, attentive, aspiring, and affectionate—such mothers *are* the special agents of God.

Notes

1. Tal D. Bonham, *The Treasury of Clean Jokes* (Nashville: Broadman Press, 1981), p. 54.

2. Wilson Wayne Grant, *The Caring Father* (Nashville: Broadman Press, 1983), pp. 12-13.

3. *Quote*, 80:247.

9
The Pushy Parent
Salome
Matthew 20:20-21

The scriptural cameos of mothers and fathers in the Bible are intriguing not merely because they relate so much about these parents of the past, but also because they leave so much unsaid. In many cases a single sentence summarizes the scope of their contribution to their children. A prime example is the mother of James and John. All we know about her role as a mother is compressed into two short verses in Matthew's Gospel. Matthew here does not even mention her name.

By turning to other verses we do pick up some further facts about her. Her husband was named Zebedee, a prominent fisherman who probably provided well for her and her boys. A careful comparison of the references in Matthew 27:56 and Mark 15:40 leads to the conclusion that her name was Salome. She is the only woman so named in Scripture.

We notice something else about her. When Jesus was hanging on the cross in his ultimate act of sacrifice, Salome stood close by. On resurrection Sunday when the women went to anoint the body of Jesus, Salome was in the group (Matt. 27:56; Mark 16:1-2). So we must conclude that she was a woman of deep faith and consuming compassion for Christ.

These positives about her, though, have been lost in the negative shadow cast by her appeal to Jesus that her sons, James and John, be granted the prime positions in his kingdom. Her request called forth a gentle rebuke from Jesus. Even worse, it has led to negative evaluation of her throughout Christian history.

But let's reexamine Salome and her request. The selfishness and presumptuousness of her request are apparent at first glance. Look deeper, however, and I believe we will discover at least three positive parental patterns we need to duplicate as parents in the twentieth century.

Importance

Behind Salome's request that James and John be granted the privilege of sitting at the right and left hand of Jesus was the recognition of the intrinsic value and worth of her boys.

From the time of Eve's exultant cry at the birth of her first son, "I have gotten a man from the Lord" (Gen. 4:1), mothers and fathers have rejoiced in their children. A child was rightly regarded as one of God's most wonderful creations, "a gift from God," (Ps. 127:3, TLB), a prize of incomparable value. Say what you will about Salome, she had at least discovered that much. Her boys were worth something. They had value. And she communicated that to them.

Somewhere along the line we have lost sight of that indispensable truth. This is evidenced by the growing number of husbands and wives who choose not to have children. A new national organization has been formed called National Organization for Non-Parenting (NON) which is propagating the cause of childlessness. Why are so many today opting for childlessness?

Part of the motivation for this new mood is concern about an overpopulated earth. That is admirable. There is at present a worldwide concern, sparked by the rapidly increasing world population and the rapidly decreasing world production. The desire to be a part of the solution, rather than to add to the problem, has motivated many not to have children.

Another part of the motivation is economic. That is also understandable. According to the latest report of the Population Reference Bureau in Washington, the out-of-pocket expense of seeing a child through birth, eighteen years under the parental roof, and four years at a public university is now $85,000 per child.[1] Common sense leads some to count the cost. Some couples intentionally remain childless because they do not judge themselves as fit prospects for parenthood and do not feel they can cope.

Part of the motivation, however, is not concern for the world population or economic concern but simple selfishness, an unwillingness to be bothered by children, an unwillingness to make the sacrifices that responsible parenthood requires. The value of a child has been lost in our narcissistic excesses.

It is not only couples without children who have lost sight of the value of a child, however. Many parents with children have also missed that important truth. The lost sense of our children's worth is seen in child abuse, a family phenomenon which has come out of the closet in recent years. According to Douglas Besharov, director of the National Center of Child Abuse and Neglect, over one million children a year are sexually abused, physically abused, or neglected to such a degree that they suffer permanent physical or psychological damage. At least one thousand a year die from this abuse.[2] Parents who abuse their children are saying, "You are of such little value and worth that I can vent my wrath and anger at the world on you."

This lost sense of our children's worth is also seen in child neglect. Many parents do not abuse their children—they simply ignore them. By putting everything else before our children in terms of our attention and time, we are tacitly communicating to them that they are not worth very much.

The attitude of our day seems to be expressed by the little girl who was asked what she thought of her new baby brother. "He's all right," she responded, "but there are a lot of things we needed worse." That is the evaluation of children that seems to prevail in our world, but Jesus proclaimed a different standard. When he declared in Matthew's Gospel, "Whoever causes one of these little ones who believe in Me to stumble, it is better for him that a heavy millstone be hung around his neck, and that he be drowned in the depth of the sea" (Matt. 18:6, NASB), Jesus was teaching that there is nothing of more value than the soul of a child who has been given into our care.

In her seemingly selfish suggestion to Jesus, Salome nevertheless revealed that she recognized the inestimable worth and value of her sons. That is a parental perception we need to perpetuate in our day.

Ideals

There is another positive element about Salome's request. When she asked Jesus if James and John could sit on his right and on his left, she was revealing she had high goals for her sons and wanted the best for them. She not only recognized the value and worth of their lives, the potential packed into each personality, but she also wanted them to realize that potential.

I recently read an article by Peter Drucker on leadership. He observed,

> Leadership is not magnetic personality—that can just as well be a glib tongue. It is not "making friends and influencing people"—that is flattery. Leadership is lifting a person's vision to higher sights, the raising of a person's performance to a higher standard, the building of a personality beyond its normal limitations.[3]

That is also a good description of the role of parents. We should continually seek to lift our children's visions to higher sights. We should constantly endeavor to raise our children's performance to a higher standard.

That's what Edith Shaeffer meant when she called the home a "birthplace of creativity." We parents are to be agents of creativity for our children. We are to create an environment for creativity, plant seeds of creativity in their lives, provide opportunities for that creativity to develop, and place before them ideals toward which that creativity can flow.[4]

General Douglas MacArthur is remembered for many reasons. I like to remember him for the prayer he prayed for his son:

> Build me a son, O Lord, who will be strong enough to know when he is weak, and brave enough to face himself when he is afraid; one who will be proud and unbending in honest defeat, and humble and gentle in victory.
>
> Build me a son whose wishbone will not be where his backbone should be; a son who will know Thee—and that to know himself is the foundation stone of knowledge.
>
> Lead him, I pray, not in the path of ease and comfort, but under the stress and spur of difficulties and challenge. Here let him learn to stand up in the storm, here let him learn compassion for those who fall.
>
> Build me a son whose heart will be clear, whose goal will be high, a son who will master himself before he seeks to master other men; one who will learn to laugh, yet never forget how to weep; one who will reach into the future, yet never forget the past.
>
> And after all these things are his, add, I pray, enough of a sense of humor, so that he may always be serious, yet never take himself too seriously. Give him humility, so that he may always remember the simplicity of true greatness, the open mind of true wisdom, the meekness of true strength.
>
> Then, I, his father, will dare to whisper, "I have not lived in vain."[5]

If we can hold out ideals for our children to strive for and encourage them to become all that they can be, then we too will not have lived in vain. That desire for her sons to reach their potential was, I believe, at the heart of Salome's request of Jesus.

Involvement

There is yet another positive aspect of Salome's request for her sons. She not only recognized the value of her sons and held out ideals before them. She also got involved in their lives in an attempt to help them realize those ideals.

The most common parental failure today is that we are too little involved in the lives of our children. Many families are like the little girl who woke up one morning about 4:00 AM. There was a violent storm outside, so the parents had moved the little girl out of her own room and put her in their bed. Then when the storm got worse, they got up and went into the kitchen. In a few moments the little girl came running into the kitchen, crying. She said, "I woke up and saw Mommy wasn't there. Then I saw Daddy wasn't there. Then I went to my bed and saw I wasn't there. And I didn't know what was going on."

I see a need in American homes for parents to *be there* enough to develop a genuine sense of intimacy with their children. An involvement in our children's lives that leads to a healthy parent-child intimacy is the greatest need in the home today.

By parent-child intimacy, I do not mean to make the child a substitute spouse. I do not imply that parents and children should have a relationship of equality. Neither do I mean that there will be complete agreement on every matter. There will always be differences of opinion between parents and their children. One mother said to her teenage daughter, "I fail to understand you," to which the daughter responded, "The failing is mutual." By parent-child intimacy I mean that we should be available to help them, encourage them, and advise them as they begin to develop that creativity within them and as they begin to move toward the ideals that are before them.

Conclusion

What would you say is the worth of a boy;
In sin and sorrow, in service and joy?
So much good or bad wrapped up in each life—
To build up and serve or tear down in strife.
A mine of diamonds, a bomb to destroy?
Depends entirely on who gets the boy!

The devil, the world, and flesh make their bid;
But what will you do to win this "kid"?
Some men have hobbies in which they invest
Much time and money with real zeal and zest
But those who fathom life's great thrills and joys
Major on making real men out of boys.[6]

Say what you will about Salome, she made real men out of
her boys because she recognized their importance, held out
high ideals before them, and became involved in their lives. All
parents should commit themselves to do likewise.

Notes

1. *Quote,* 80:316.
2. *Quote,* 77:220.
3. *Quote,* 80:339.
4. Edith Schaeffer, *What Is a Family?* (Old Tappan, New Jersey: Fleming
H. Revell Co., 1975), p. 54 ff.
5. Wayne E. Warner, comp., *1000 Stories and Quotations of Famous
People* (Grand Rapids: Baker Book House, 1972), p. 222.
6. Author unknown, quoted in James C. Hefley, *A Dictionary of Illustrations* (Grand Rapids: Zondervan Publishing House, 1971), pp. 43-44.

10
The Passionate Parent
The Possessed Boy's Father
Mark 9:14-29

A young man planning a pastoral ministry was talking with an older pastor about the challenges and opportunities which were ahead. One aspect of the ministry which especially fascinated the young minister-to-be was conducting a wedding ceremony. Therefore, he listened carefully as the experienced pastor went through each step with the most infinite care and meticulous detail. He concluded his comments by advising, "If you ever forget what to say, just quote Scripture. It is always appropriate to quote Scripture."

Soon the young man was ordained, and his first opportunity came to perform a wedding ceremony. Nervously he rehearsed the details in his mind and then walked out into the sanctuary to begin the service. All went well until he pronounced the couple husband and wife. He forgot what to say next. His mind went blank. Suddenly he remembered the advice of the dear old pastor, "Quote Scripture." He decided to try it. Unfortunately the only Scripture he could think of, which he dutifully quoted, was, "Father, forgive them; for they do not know what they are doing" (Luke 23:34, NASB).

That prayer could be pronounced over many homes today. Many parents are ineffective and unsuccessful in their parenting roles because they know not what they do. Not only do we need to pray, "Father, forgive us," but we also need to pray that God will help us do better. We need not only to acknowledge the problem but also to do something about it. We need to find some helpful, healthy parental models from which to gain inspiration and instruction.

This book has presented models of biblical parents from whose successes and failures we can learn. In this chapter we'll look at an unnamed father who had a unique encounter with Jesus. The story of this encounter appears with only slight variations in Mark 9, Matthew 17, and Luke 9. Although our basic text is Mark 9, we will draw from all of them. Here we see a concerned father who provides a parental model for us today. Let's look at him more closely.

Priority

He was a concerned father because he gave priority to his responsibility as a parent. We see this in several aspects of the story.

The very fact that this father was traveling the countryside with his disturbed son, seeking to find help, indicates a deep commitment on that father's part. He could have left it for the wife to do. He could have alibied to his wife, as many fathers do today, "I will take care of things at work. The home and children are your responsibility." He could have ignored the problem, or he could have recognized the problem but accepted it as an inevitable part of their lives.

These are common approaches of fathers in our day. The father in our story, though, followed none of those cop-outs. Instead, after recognizing that there was a problem with his son he traveled everywhere seeking a miracle worker, a pious saint of God who could make his boy well. All other responsibilities fell in line behind his concern for the well-being of his son. Here was a father who gave priority to his parental responsibility.

The concern of the father was also shown in the intensity of his language. The version of the story in Luke 9 makes this clear. When the man came to Jesus he said, "Master, I beseech thee, look upon my son" (v. 38). That word *beseech* is a strong word. It is the word used in Luke 5:12 when a man with leprosy saw Jesus and "besought" Jesus to heal him. Nothing was as important as being rid of his leprosy.

It is the word used in Acts 21:39 when Paul was seized by the mob and about to be killed. He said, "I beseech thee, suffer me to speak." It was a matter of life and death.

It is the word employed in Acts 26:3. Standing before Agrippa, Paul recognized his tremendous opportunity to bear a crucial witness for Christ, so he said, "I beseech thee to hear me patiently." It was a once in a lifetime opportunity.

It is the word utilized in Galatians 4:12 where Paul could see his entire life's work in danger of slipping away into a Judaistic legalism that would undermine the gospel. So he said, "Brethren, I beseech you, become as I am" (RSV).

Every time that word is used in the New Testament it expresses an intensity of desire, an urgency of purpose, a priority of concern. So it is in this story. It was as if the man were saying to Jesus, "Master, nothing else matters to me as much as this. Nothing else is important if I can't find help at this point. I beseech you, Lord, please help my son." It was a matter of top priority.

I wonder, can that be said about your commitment as a father? As a parent? Is it a high-priority item in your life? Is it at the top of the list on your personal agenda?

Is succeeding as a parent as serious as succeeding in your work? Are you as careful about your investments in your children's lives as you are about your investments in stocks and bonds? Do you spend as much time developing your children as you do your tennis game? Does parenting really matter to you?

The first principle in successful parenting, the clearest demonstration that you are a concerned parent, is to give top priority to your responsibility as a parent.

Perception

We notice another factor in the story. The man who had a unique encounter with Jesus accurately perceived what his son's problem was. The father had perception.

Tremendous debate has ensued about the illnesses in the New Testament. The three different accounts of this story reflect these differences of opinion. Mark states that the boy was possessed with a spirit (Mark 9:17, NASB). Luke records that he was seized by a spirit (Luke 9:39). Matthew writes that the boy was an epileptic (Matt. 17:15).

Were these afflicted people in the New Testament really demon possessed? I believe personally that in this particular instance the boy had a physical problem, epilepsy, which was described in spiritual terms, demon possession.

What I want you to see is this: the father knew exactly what the boy's problem was and could describe how it affected the boy in the most accurate detail. This father was not one who occasionally glanced at his son as their lives passed each other like two ships in the night. Instead, he was a father who, through his involvement in his son's life, had a personal perception of what his son's needs were.

One of the most obviously missing ingredients in today's home is a sensitivity on the part of parents to their children's needs, problems, desires, pressures, and levels of development. We don't really know our children. A popular phrase in recent days is, "It is now twelve o'clock, parents. Do you know where your children are?" Take the question a step further and ask, "Do you know where your children are emotionally? Do you know where your children are spiritually? Do you know where your children are intellectually? Do you know where your children are?"

Several years ago, the *Pennsylvania State Law Enforcement Journal* quoted a letter from a runaway son. The parents begged their son to come home, but he refused. He wrote a letter to explain why. The letter said in part:

> Remember when I was about six or seven and I used to want you to just listen to me? I remember all the nice things you gave me for Christmas and my birthday and I was really happy with the things—about a week—at the time I got the things, but the rest of the time during the year I really didn't want presents. I just wanted all the time for you to listen to me like I was somebody who felt things too, because I remember even when I was young I felt things. But you said you were busy.
>
> Mom, you are a wonderful cook, and you have everything so clean and you were tired so much from doing all those things that made you busy; but, you know something, Mom? I would have liked crackers and peanut butter just as well if you had only sat down with me a while during the day and said to me: "Tell me all about it so I can maybe help you understand." . . .
>
> If anybody asks you where I am, tell them I've gone looking for somebody with time because I've got a lot of things I want to talk about.

A concerned father is one who spends enough time with his children to listen and share so that he can really get to know who they are. Perception.

Planning

He was a concerned father also because he made the necessary plans to deal with his son's need. He was not only aware of his son's need, but he did something about it.

I read recently a discussion about the church's ministry to single adults. An interesting phrase grabbed my attention. "Many churches treat single adults as second class Christians," the man wrote, "not because they mean to but because they don't plan not to."[1]

Let me paraphrase that statement and apply it to the home. Many parents let their children down not because they mean to, but because they don't plan not to. Think how carefully you plan your day's activities and how casually you plan your role as a parent. Think how meticulously you map out the journey you will follow on your summer vacation and how indifferently you relate to your child's journey through life. Think how scrupulously you plan your financial investment and how lackadaisically you make your investments in your children.

When NASA set out to put a man on the moon, a vital part of its program was contingency planning. That is, the project leaders anticipated every possible situation that could go wrong. They analyzed every potential problem and the proper response in each case. NASA simply refused to be surprised. How much contingency planning do you do concerning your children?

Someone has said, "Family life is an existential classroom; it lasts for about eighteen years."[2] The tragedy is that most parents attempt this teaching without any lesson plans.

A concerned father is one who knows what his children's needs are and who carefully and thoroughly makes plans for those needs to be met.

Perseverance

This concerned father shows us that a key ingredient in successful parenting is perseverance.

How many others this father had taken his son to see we do not know, but notice what happened in the story. Verse 18 states that the man brought his son to the disciples to be healed, and they could not do it. What did the father do? Did he give up? Did he quit trying? Did he go home? No. The father stayed until he could see Jesus. He absolutely would not give up until he had exhausted every possible alternative.

Mark Twain often chided himself for his gullibility as an investor. He wrote checks to support hundreds of inventions which never succeeded. Finally, after continuous discouragement, he decided he had learned his lesson. He turned down the next young inventor with a "definitely and positively not." The young man's name was Alexander Graham Bell. His invention was a talking machine called the telephone.

That is a parable of parenting. We make investment after investment until finally, in dreadful discouragement, we give up. But it may be the very next investment which brings the dividend, the very next investment of time, concern, love, attention, or prayer that will effect the change. So whatever you do as a parent, don't ever give up. Success is often determined by our willingness to persevere.

Conclusion

We live in a day of tremendous challenge to the family. The tide will be turned and the challenge met when we have Christian fathers and mothers who become concerned enough about their responsibilities to decide:

1. We will give top priority to our roles as parents;

2. We will be sensitive enough to our children to perceive what their needs are;

3. We will carefully and prayerfully plan to meet those needs; and

4. We will stay at it until the job is done.

Notes

1. Michael R. Tucker, *The Church that Dared to Change* (Wheaton: Illinois: Tyndale House Publishers, 1975), p. 53.

2. Quoted in Gordon MacDonald, *The Effective Father* (Wheaton: Tyndale House Publishers, 1977), p. 27.

11
The Productive Parent
Eunice
2 Timothy 1:5

What determines how a child will turn out? What is the primary force which molds the life of an individual and determines what he will accomplish in life?

It is obviously not geographic location, for productive people and parasites of society both come from all places.

Educational opportunities are not the answer. There are enough Ph.D.'s in prison to staff any college.

Neither is denominational affiliation the key. When Billy Graham preached once at a prison, the warden leaned over and said, "It might comfort you to know that fifty percent of our inmates are Baptists." Some comfort!

Sheer talent is not the secret. There are talented crooks as well as talented Christians.

Even circumstances do not seem to be the key factor, for some of life's most productive citizens have come out of the most unpleasant circumstances.

What then most determines what a child will become? I believe that the answer is the child's parents. Like no other factor in a child's life, the parents will determine his point of view in life. Like father, like son. Like mother, like daughter. That truth looms large in human history.

Often our parental influence is negative. Upon his return from a visit to the zoo, the child related his adventure to his mother. "I saw a giraffe with a neck a mile long!" he declared. His mother chided with this response, "I've told you a million times not to exaggerate!" I wonder where he learned to exaggerate.

A father was welcomed home by his distraught wife. She complained about the filthy language her son had used. Angrily, the father started up the stairs to the boy's room. "I'll teach that boy to curse!" the father shouted. On the fifth step, he stepped on a skate which the boy had accidentally left on the step. His foot slipped, and he fell back down the steps. As the father was falling, he let loose with a string of curse words. He was greeted at the bottom of the steps by his wife who said, "Come on back into the kitchen. That's enough words for his first lesson!" I wonder where that boy learned to curse.

At other times, our parental influence is positive. So it was for the parent we are considering in this chapter. This biblical mother passed on her faith to her son. Eunice was her name, and she is mentioned in only one verse in the New Testament. Yet, that one brief reference has emblazoned her name with immortality and exalted her to a place of preeminence. For what is she exalted? Did she start a church? Was she a dynamic missionary? Was she an outstanding author? A successful Christian businesswoman? No, none of the above. She became a heroine of the Bible and was honored as one of God's dear saints because she passed on her faith to her son.

The fact of her accomplishment becomes even more amazing when we understand the circumstances of her life. The Bible indicates that Eunice, a Jew, married a Gentile, with whom she did not share a common faith (Acts 16:1). Why Eunice was willing to become unequally yoked with an unbeliever we do not know. The point is that she did. Eunice was not a mother who had the help of a supportive, committed husband who was willing to give spiritual leadership in the home. Rather, she had to do it all on her own.

An early tradition arose which suggested that Eunice was widowed while Timothy was still young. If so, she had to carry the load of being both father and mother to her son. That is, she was a single parent.

Parenting was not easy for Eunice. Yet, here was a woman who dared to stand up in the face of unpleasant circumstances and succeed at life's most challenging task—the task of parenthood.

How did she do it? What were the practices that enabled Eunice to pass on her faith to her son?

She Planted It

The first obvious factor in the story of Eunice and her son, Timothy, is that she planted the faith in his life at an early age. From the first day of his life, he had a constant reminder of the importance of faith, and that reminder was his name. She named him Timothy, which meant "God-fearing."

Eunice could not put the fruit of faith in her son's life. She knew that, but she could plant the seeds which she hoped someday would blossom into faith. She could not make him reverence God, but she could give him that name to live up to. The process of passing on her faith to her son began the day he was born.

In our day there is a reaction against this practice. In the name of tolerance we usually declare, "I'm not going to force faith on my child. I'm not going to influence him in matters of religion. I'm going to let him make up his own mind."

That sounds awfully tolerant. Strangely, the area of religion is the only area where we show such universal tolerance.

If your child sasses you, you don't say, "I'm not going to force my behavior pattern on my child. I'm not going to influence him in his manners. I'm going to let him make up his own mind how to act." That's not what you say. Instead, you say, "You better straighten up your sassy mouth, or it's going to be all over for you!" What happened to our tolerance?

If a child refuses to go to school, you don't say, "I'm not

going to force my educational pattern on my child. I'm going to let him make up his own mind." Instead, you say something like this: "If you don't get yourself out that door and headed toward school before I count to three, you're going to be sorry." What happened to our tolerance?

When your child refuses to eat good food and instead comes walking in with a piece of cake in each hand and saying, "At last I'm getting a balanced meal," you don't say, "I'm not going to force my eating habits on my child. I'm going to let him make up his own mind." Rather, you say, "Put that cake down. We're going to eat supper in five minutes, and you're not getting up from the table until you have eaten everything on your plate."

We parents, in every area of life, hopefully want what is best for our children. So we try to determine what is best, and then we go about planting the ideas and developing the personal habits that will enable our children to realize the best, to experience fulfillment. If we do that in the areas of personal behavior, education, diet, and grooming, why shouldn't we do it in the spiritual realm?

When you do plant the seeds of faith in the life of your child, when you don't create a kind of spiritual climate in your home that will influence your child in matters of religion, you are not being tolerant. You are being negligent.

One writer suggests that Christian parenthood is a war against the forces which would destroy our children's lives. He explains,

> The prize is the inner spirit of my children, and the stakes are high. Arrayed against me are those who wish to extract money, loyalty, and the strong creative energy my son or daughter may have to give. In the eternal dimension, the prize is the soul of my children. I am not prepared to compromise or negotiate. Until my children are old and wise enough to distinguish their enemies from their friends, I hold the responsibility to conduct both a defense and an offense on their behalf.[1]

Eunice was able to pass on her faith to her son because she started the day he was born by planting the seeds of faith in his life. She fought the battle against those forces that would destroy her son from day one.

She Taught It

We notice a second factor. Not only did she plant the faith in Timothy's life at the beginning, but she also taught him the faith as he grew up. We see this not in our text but in 2 Timothy 3:14-15 where Paul wrote: "You, however, continue in the things you have learned and become convinced of, knowing from whom you have learned them; and that from childhood you have known the sacred writings which are able to give you the wisdom that leads to salvation through faith which is in Christ Jesus" (NASB). Paul said of Timothy, "from childhood you have known the sacred writings."

Can that be said about your children, that from childhood they have known the Bible and what it says? That means that you need to help your children faithfully attend Sunday School and worship. But it means more than that.

Lyle Schaller, in his book *Understanding Tomorrow,* identifies one of the characteristics of our age to be excessive expectations of institutions. To a substantial degree, we parents have turned over to two institutions, the school and the church, the responsibility of helping our children grow up into dedicated, dependable adults. Test after test, however, has revealed that these expectations placed on our institutions far exceed their capabilities. We parents simply cannot delegate to other institutions the responsibilities that must be carried out in the home. These institutions are to supplement what we do in the home, not replace what we should do in the home.[2]

If your children are to learn to love God, you have to teach them. If they are to become men and women of faith, you have to develop them. If they are to know from childhood the sacred Scriptures, it will be because you have committed yourself to teaching the Bible in the home.

To pass our faith on to our children we must teach them the faith, as revealed in the Word of God in our home. That was the secret of Eunice's success.

She Lived It

Eunice planted the faith in Timothy's life. Then she taught the faith to him, and third, she lived it.

Paul speaks in our text of the "unfeigned" faith of Eunice and her mother (KJV). The *New American Standard Bible* translates the word "sincere." Phillips has it "genuine faith." The Greek word derives from a verb from which we get our word *hypocrite*. A hypocrite was one who acted beneath a guise, an actor who wore a mask and played a part. Paul says of Eunice's faith that it was unhypocritical. It was not a put-on faith. It was for real. What this means is that the faith Eunice claimed to have publicly she also lived privately. She lived her faith at home.

How important it is for us to understand that, because the single most powerful impact that you have on your children is not what you say but what you do, not the convictions you claim to have but the convictions you really have as evidenced by the way you live your life.

Be a real person at home. Be genuine in your religious commitment. Don't make a show of your religion, but in the day-by-day relationships of your family life, let your religion show. Children will know if their parents are phonies. And phony parents produce phony children.

The secret of Eunice's success in passing on her faith to her son was that she lived out her faith in a genuine, sincere way in her home. She lived it.

Conclusion

How is the transition made from the faith of the parents to the faith of the child? Cecil Osborne beautifully illustrates with the example of a person who inherits the house of his parents. The individual decides to live in the house. As he revisits the home, he discovers an unsatisfying mixture of furniture of several different styles and from several different eras. He tries shifting the furniture around, but he is still not satisfied. Finally, he takes all the furniture outside. After studying it, he selects several pieces which he wants to keep. Some he puts in the living room, some in the bedroom, and so on. Finally, the house is about half furnished with the inherited furniture that he likes. Then, he goes shopping for the additional pieces needed to furnish the house completely. After the new furniture has been put into place, and the house repainted, the house has become *his* house.

So it is with the faith of our parents. The fundamental elements will be inherited from your parents. But only after the faith of your parents has been studied, reexamined, and then adapted to your own needs will that faith really become yours.[3]

Eunice provided Timothy with the basic ingredients of a religious faith. From what he inherited, he added his own unique understanding. The result was a personal faith that was genuinely his. But the basic elements he received from his mother, for she was a parent who cared enough about her son to pass on her faith to him.

Notes

1. Gordon McDonald, *The Effective Father* (Wheaton, Illinois: Tyndale House Publishers, 1977), p. 40.

2. Lyle E. Schaller, *Understanding Tomorrow* (Nashville: Abingdon Press, 1976), pp. 46-49.

3. Cecil G. Osborne, *The Art of Becoming a Whole Person* (Waco: Word Books, 1978), p. 55.

12
The Patient Parent
The Prodigal's Father
Luke 15:11-31

The story of the prodigal son in Luke 15 is one of the most famous narratives ever told. Jesus related this story, no doubt, to illustrate the love of God (represented by the father) for sinners (represented by the two sons). But let's approach it from a different perspective. Let's see the man in the story as a representative not of our Heavenly Father but of an earthly father who struggled to develop a healthy relationship with two radically different sons. As I studied the story from this perspective, I discovered that this man provided a beautiful model for parents of today. Notice some insights into parenting that the prodigal's father gives us.

Flexible

The confrontation pictured in verse 12 is one that usually occurs in every home. On the one hand are parents who have been providing the needs and making the decisions for their child. On the other hand is the child who has reached the point where he wants to care for his own needs and make his own decisions. How you handle that confrontation as a parent will determine the quality of your relationship with your child. You have two options before you.

One option is control. Controlling parents make all the decisions, do all the work, and meet all the needs of their children—refusing to recognize the developing potential within the child for self-discipline and self-sufficiency.

The other option is a flexibility that will enable you to let your child go. This is the option modeled for us by the father in our text.

This flexible father realized that parenthood was not a permanent position. That realization is not easy to accept, but it is true nevertheless. From the beginning, we are preparing our children to leave us. They will not always be small, young, and dependent. They will not always be with us. Consequently, a model parent is one who equips the child for life so that when he leaves, he will be prepared and we will be ready for the separation.

How can we do that?

1. *Responsibility*

One important step is to provide responsibilities for our children commensurate with their ability. Weary of the constant disorder in her son's room, one mother laid down the law. For every item she had to pick up off the floor, he would have to pay her a nickel. At the end of a week, the boy owed her 65 cents. She received the money promptly—along with a 50-cent tip and a note which said, "Thanks, Mom. Keep up the good work!"

A child who grows up with parents who do everything for him will never learn to do things for himself. When he moves out into the world, he will be unable to cope with the realities of life.

One father expressed it like this: "If a youngster is to survive and prosper outside the family cocoon, by age 13 a blast of cold air should be let in. The child must begin to see that not all his needs are going to be tended automatically."[1] A flexible parent is one who provides responsibilities for children which will help them develop to the point where they can take care of themselves.

2. *Relationships*

Another important step is to perceive relationships with your children according to their personalities. Every child is different. We see this in our text. One of the man's sons was an adventurer, one who liked the excitement of new challenges, one who was willing to take risks. The other was a homebody, one who liked the security of the familiar, one who did not like to go out on a limb. They were brothers, but they were radically different in their personalities.

Not only are children different in their personalities, but their relationship within the family also creates within them a different outlook.

Two researchers recently published their findings on the birth order of children and how that affects personality. Firstborns, they reported, have a need to be right. They feel a sense of responsibility for what goes on in their families and will be more like their fathers than their mothers. Secondborns tune into the underlying emotional needs of the family and will often identify with their mothers. Thirdborns don't form strong alliances with either parent individually and will connect with the marriage itself. They make good mediators. Fourth kids will identify with the family as a whole and, if there is too much underlying tension, will virtually absorb it all. Fourthborns may feel overwhelmed at times. Fifthborns duplicate many of the characteristics of firstborns, and the cycle starts over again.[2]

No set of instructions or approach will work with all children, because they are different. A flexible parent is one who recognizes these differences, and relates to each child uniquely according to the perceived needs of that child.

3. *Risk*

A flexible parent is also willing to permit risks for our children according to their durability.

A child psychologist provided this perceptive insight into effective parenting. He said,

> If there is a single concept which best distinguishes an effective from an ineffective parent it is this. A poor parent is one who intervenes between a child's behavior and the consequences of

that behavior. A good parent is one who allows a child to experience the consequences of his acts.[3]

Nowhere is this truth more beautifully illustrated than in our text. When the young boy came to his father and said, "Daddy, give me what is mine. I'm going to make my own way," the father knew that it was a risk. He knew that there were people who could hurt his son, supposed friends who would take advantage of him, and situations that would cause pain for him. But he let him go. Why? Because he knew that such risks were a necessary part of developing the boy into adulthood.

Don't minimize the disappointment the boy experienced or the despair he felt as he went into the far country, lost his money, was forsaken by his friends, and ended up in the slop of the pigpen. Those disappointments were real. But the remarkable thing about the story is that the pain and agony of failure became the crucible in which that boy was molded into a man.

There are basically two options open to you as a parent. You can control your children in a kind of smother love which so shelters them that they are unable to develop into mature, self-sufficient adults. Or, you can be flexible enough to provide the responsibilities and perceive the relationships and permit the risks that will equip them to face life.

The father in our story is a model of the kind of flexibility that will enable us to let our children go.

Faithful

We see a second truth about parenting in the prodigal's father. He was not only flexible. He was also faithful. We see this illustrated in verse 20.

For months, maybe for years, the young man lived in the far country. He had belittled his father's honor. He had betrayed his father's heritage. He had broken his father's heart. He had made mockery of everything that his father stood for. Yet, the picture painted in verse 20 tells us that his father never stopped loving him.

Something happened to the boy in the slop of the pigpen. "He came to himself," the Bible says (v. 17). He decided that it would be better to be a slave of his father than a slave to his passions, so he got up and headed back home. Notice what verse 20 says, "But while he was still a long way off, his father saw him, and felt compassion for him" (NASB).

Probably not a day had gone by that the father had not scanned the horizon to see if he could catch a glimpse of the profile of his son, coming back home. On that dramatic day, when he actually saw his son, this father ran out to communicate to his son that no matter what happened, he still loved him.

A model parent is one who communicates to children that they can never do anything to destroy that love. The knowledge of that love, planted in the hearts of children, will keep them going in the difficult times of their lives.

A World War II aviator was downed in the North Sea during bitter winter weather. Day after day he clung to his safety raft in spite of the winds, the sleet, and the mountainlike waves of that sea of sudden storms and vicious weather. At last he was rescued. One of the rescuers asked him how he had ever held out for so long under such adverse conditions. He answered, "I could never have done it except for the fact that I knew I was being sought."[4]

Our children will go through much stormy weather in their lifetimes, but if they know deep down on the inside that we love them regardless; that no matter what they do or how they fail or how far they fall, we will still love them—then that will be the single ingredient that will enable them to hold on.

The father in our story is a model of the kind of faithful love that will enable our children to hold on during difficult times.

Forgiving

A third insight from the prodigal's father is seen in the homecoming experience with his son. Verse 20 reveals the faithfulness of the father's love. Verse 22 reveals the forgiving quality of his love.

In verse 21, the boy acknowledged his sin. "Father, I have sinned against heaven and in your sight; I am no longer worthy to be called your son" (NASB). That is a world of difference from the arrogant young man who had demanded his share of the inheritance and had gone off to squander it in the far country. He felt that he had forfeited his right to be a son. Consequently, he would be satisfied in simply being a servant in the household of his father.

But notice what the father did in verse 22. When he called for the robe and ring, symbols of sonship, he was declaring that the past with all its failures and misunderstandings was behind them. He restored the prodigal to his position as a son. Because he loved his son, he was willing to give him a second chance.

Louisa Fletcher Tarkington has expressed the wishes of us all when she wrote:

> I wish that there were some wonderful place
>   In the land of beginning Again;
> Where all our mistakes and all our heartaches
>   And all of our poor selfish grief
> Could be dropped like a shabby old coat at the door
>   And never put on again.

If there is anything a home ought to be it is a place of beginning again, a place where we can forget the hurts and forgive the slights and forge the problems of yesterday into the possibilities of tomorrow. If there is anything a home ought to be it is a place where we can say to each other, "You're not OK and I'm not OK and that's OK!"

The father in our story is a model of the kind of forgiveness that will allow us to move beyond the failures of yesterday and help our children begin again today.

Favorable

The prodigal's father was flexible in dealing with his sons, faithful in his love, and forgiving in his spirit. One more insight needs to be mentioned. This biblical father was also favorable. He was willing to make all of his resources available to his son as the son rebuilt his life and developed himself into the person God wanted him to be.

In his book *Is There a Family in the House?* Ken Chafin suggests four pictures of the family. The family is a place to grow people, a center for creativity, a place of safety and security, and a transmitter of values.[5]

How can your family and my family become that kind of place?

It will happen when we see the family as a life support system and not as a blame society.

It will happen when we begin to give our home first place in our priorities instead of last place.

It will happen when we begin to give of ourselves unreservedly so that, like the model father in Jesus' story, we are willing to make all our resources available to each other as we build our lives according to the purpose and plan of God.

Years ago, when Sir Christopher Wren was building Saint Paul's Cathedral in London, Wren was making a tour of the building. He asked a man working on the building, "What are you doing?" The workman replied, "I am cutting this stone to the right size."

He asked a second man, "What are you doing?" "I am earning a living," came the retort.

Wren came to a third man and asked the identical question. "What are you doing?" The man paused for a moment, and then in great excitement responded, "I'm helping Sir Christopher Wren build Saint Paul's Cathedral!"[6]

Ask some parents what they are doing, and some will respond, "I'm just getting by." Some will respond, "I'm just doing my job." But others, captured by the possibilities of parenthood, will say with genuine commitment, "I am helping God build a life!" May the Lord increase their tribe!

Notes

1. J. D. Sanderson, "Adult at Eighteen," *Reader's Digest,* March, 1977, p. 136.

2. *Quote,* 79:100.

3. Logan Wright, *Parent Power* (New York: William Morrow & Company, Inc., 1980), p. 144.

4. Charles L. Wallis, ed., *The Minister's Manual, 1981* (San Francisco: Harper & Row, 1981), p. 239.

5. Kenneth Chafin, *Is There a Family in the House?* (Waco: Word Books, 1978), pp. 18-28.

6. John A. MacArthur, Jr., *The Church: The Body of Christ* (Grand Rapids: Zondervan, 1973), p. 198.

Postscript

A little Sunday School girl, describing the event of creation, commented, "First God created Adam. Then he looked at him and said, 'I think I can do better than that if I tried again.' So he created Eve." Whether or not that was exactly the way it happened, the Bible indicates that when these two were created—man and woman—they joined together in the establishment of a home, the two having become one. "Therefore," says the Bible, "shall a man leave his father and his mother, and shall cleave unto his wife: and they shall be one flesh" (Gen. 2:24).

From that day until ours, individuals have accepted this challenge and, in various forms and according to various customs, have left their parents' homes in which they were reared and have formed their own homes and have reared their own families.

The family is man's oldest institution. Said one authority, "The nuclear family, consisting of an approved association between a man, at least one woman, and their children, is found as a recognizable unit in every known society"; and he adds, "It may be that men have lived in families as long as men have been men."[1] Throughout the centuries there has always been the family.

But what of the family today, in our century? What faces the split-level family in the space age?

The Changing

The first obvious fact is that the family today is confronted by change. This is not new, in itself. But the degree of change and the swiftness with which the change comes are greater today than perhaps ever before. Of the many changes that face the home, at least three seem to be of greatest significance.

1. *Mobilization*

One of these changes is mobilization. We have become a society on the move. A couple of generations ago, an individual would more commonly live his life surrounded by relatives and friends that he had known since childhood. The same physician who helped to deliver him would attend him for years. He would belong to the church that his great-grandparents had founded. And he would be buried in his family plot as his ancestors before him.

Today, things have changed. America is now a mobile society. The latest figures indicate that forty million people moved last year. That means that one out of every five persons in our nation lives in a different place now than a year ago. The 1970 census indicated that half of the people of our nation have been at their present address less than five years.[2]

What is the result?

We are thrown into strange situations with different people, facing forced adaptation to new surroundings. The resulting cultural shock, loneliness, and moral confusion which accompany such mobilization are major causes of the instability of the family in the space age.

2. *Emancipation*

Another change facing the family in the space age is the emancipation of women. One man's description of the woman's role as inspiring the spouse, training the sprigs, and cooking the sprouts is no longer accurate. In 1971, nearly one-half (43 percent) of the nation's mothers worked outside the home. One of three mothers with children under six is working today.[3]

This emancipation of womanhood, while it has been too slow in coming and in many cases has positive results, also causes some distinctive problems within the family. The sexual and affectional life of the couple may be affected. Very few women can work eight hours, come home and do the housework, wash the clothes, cook the meal, deal with the children, and then jump in bed at 10:00 and be Sexy Susie. Children might be resentful of not having more of mothers' time and indeed in some cases may be neglected. Often the wife has to work two shifts—on the job and then at home—if her husband will not give a helping hand. This adds to her fatigue and frustration.

Her financial independence may lead to conflict with her husband over matters of finance. One spokesman said, "It is my firm conviction, after dealing with hundreds of marital problems over about thirty years, that a large factor in the increase in divorce is due to the economic emancipation of women."[4]

In addition, the emancipation of woman has often led to role changes within the home which at times have caused confusion. A leading Eastern Seaboard physician and mental health specialist claimed at the Academy of Psychosomatic Medicine a few years ago that the rising incidence of sexual frigidity in wives, sexual impotency in husbands, and homosexuality in children is largely due to "role change," that is, women and men exchanging their part in society and home.[5]

3. *Liberalization*

A third major change confronting the family today is liberalization. We have seen in our time a tremendous change in the social mores and legal decrees of our nation. Laws have been passed which are much more liberal in the areas of abortion, adoption, and divorce which drastically affect the complexion of family life. Changing moral standards, a new openness in the sexual dimension, growing pressures from pornography peddlers, a new boldness among homosexuals—all of these are marks of the liberalization trend.

Recently I saw a special feature on television about a surrogate mother who lived somewhere on the East Coast. She had been artificially inseminated and was carrying a baby for a family in Kentucky. When she delivered the baby, the baby would be given to the family in Kentucky. In return for her services, this surrogate mother would be paid ten thousand dollars. No better illustration than that can be given to affirm that things are changing in family life.

When we consider the split-level family in the space age the first thing we all have to admit is that things are changing.

The Challenge

When confronted by the changes of mobilization, emancipation, and liberalization, what can we do? What is our challenge?

1. *Accept*

We must recognize the inevitability of change. The universe testifies to the reality of change. History reminds us of the futility of those who stubbornly try to resist all change simply because it is different from what went before.

2. *Adjust*

We must seek to use this change creatively. Our first evaluation of change is always that it is a threat, and our first reaction is to resist it.

We all feel that way. What we need to realize is that all change is not necessarily for the worse. Some of it can be used constructively if we adjust to it properly.

Changes such as the shorter workweek can provide more opportunity for family-centered projects if the time is used wisely.

Changed attitudes toward sex can be the opening we need to teach sex education where it should be taught—in the home. One youngster asked his mother where he came from, and she gave him a tall tale about a beautiful, white-feathered bird that brought him from heaven. He asked where she came from, and she told him the same story. He went to his grandmother and asked where she came from, and she said that the stork brought her. The boy went outside to his friends and said, "My family is really weird. There hasn't been a normal birth in our family in three generations." The new openness will give us the opportunity to tell our children that the stork is dead and then to begin training them with a true understanding.

Increased mobility can be used to broaden the cultural knowledge and appreciation of our children.

Even the economic pinch which has settled upon our nation can draw us closer together as a family and force us to use our minds to think of new and inexpensive ways to enjoy each other's company.

The challenge for the family today is to face the change, to accept it, and to deal with it creatively.

3. *Accentuate*

The third challenge is to retain the things that should not be changed. There are some factors relating to family life that must not change. These are the changeless in the midst of the changing, the anchor in the midst of the rolling waves, the cornerstone in the house that must remain firm and constant. It is imperative that we continue to accentuate the four basic functions of the home.

The *sustaining function* must not change. According to the biblical account of creation, the primary purpose of marriage is companionship (Gen. 2:18,22). There was a part of Adam, a need in his life, an emptiness in the depth of his soul that was not complete until he found a woman who could be a "help meet" for him and provide the fellowship which he so desperately needed.

Someone has said that man is not complete until he is married, and then he is finished. The latter may be true in some cases, but the former is true. Man is incomplete without the fellowship and companionship of other people. One of the primary functions of the home is that it provides a stable source of support by which we are sustained in life.

The tragedy of the family in the space age is that this sustaining function has often been discarded. Many husbands and wives who live together and raise families together are not really friends. Nor do they sustain each other. Instead of support in the home, there is suspicion. Instead of understanding, there is unconcern. Instead of empathy, there is apathy. Instead of companionship, there is combat. Marital bliss has changed to marital blisters. The sustaining function has been lost.

But it is here that we must plant our feet against the tide of change and retain in the home this sustaining function which provides love and acceptance and support and encouragement. What most human beings, young or old, need in this world more than anything else is encouragement. It is the home which God has provided to meet that need. That must not change.

The *sexual function* of the home must not change. This is being strongly challenged today by the playboy philosophy, the increase in premarital sex, increased infidelity, and trial marriage—all of which go under the guise of the new morality. According to the last US Census the number of couples living together unmarried skyrocketed by more than 700 percent from 1960 to 1970.[6]

Why has this happened? Because we are being captured by the claim that "everyone is doing it." I want to suggest today that right and wrong is not determined by the practice of the majority but by the purpose of God. And the Bible makes it unmistakably clear that the divine purpose for sex was for it to be experienced in a family situation between a man and

woman who love each other so much that they don't care
about loving anyone else in quite the same way and have thus
committed themselves permanently to each other in marriage.
Positively, this provides for the procreation of new lives, it
provides for the establishment of lasting relationships, and it
provides a healthy environment for the expression of our
sexuality. Negatively, it protects against the sometimes irre-
parable psychological damage and unbearable guilt of uncon-
trolled and unguided sexual urges.

The sexual function of the home must not change, for sex
demands the total blending of two personalities. It demands
security for the woman. It demands responsibility for the man.
And it demands publicity. Outside of marriage you do not have
security, you don't have publicity, you don't have responsibility. You have only an isolated and perverted part of a beautiful
whole; and you cannot end up with anything but frustration,
confusion, and conflicts. The home must remain as the proper
arena for intimate sexual relationships. That must not change.

The *social function* of the home must not change. As I
quoted earlier, Fosdick once said that the home "is a hothouse
where in a certain isolation of sheltered loyalties beautiful
things are grown—affections, sympathies, insights, devotions—which afterwards can be transplanted and applied to
the common good of mankind."[7] What an ideal for the home
to live up to! What a positive force it could have in the world if
it were a hothouse where beautiful things were grown. What a
power the home would be if in it we trained our children to be
responsible citizens, loving husbands and wives, dedicated
parents, and hardworking employees.

What does it mean?

This means that the home is a place for training. The writer
of Proverbs speaks of the home as a school in which children
are to be taught. And we parents are the teachers.

It also means that the home is a place for love. The home
should be permeated with love which is not so much talked

about as shown, not so much taught as caught.

In addition, this means that the home is to be a place for discipline. Grady Wilson, the evangelist, was asked if his mother ever spanked him. He said, "She had a strap in the kitchen which hung under the motto, 'I need thee every hour.'"

The home is the place where your children are to be prepared for life. That socializing function of the home must not change.

In addition, the *spiritual function* of the home must not change.

Our challenge as parents is to help our children develop a solid concept of God, to put the hands of our children in the hand of their Heavenly Father. No matter what else we do for our children—if we bring them up in the most beautiful home, if we feed them the best food, if we dress them in the finest clothes, if we send them to the most famous schools, if we establish them in the most prominent job—if we do all that and have not given them a spiritual heritage upon which they can build their lives, then we have really not given them anything at all.

The Conclusion

It is my firm conviction that help for facing the challenges of family life today can be discovered in the Word of God and the models presented there. These ancient models are amazingly relevant to our time. I hope that these parental models will enable you to do a better job at what is still life's most challenging task, even in the space age—the task of parenting.

Notes

1. D. Elton & Pauline Trueblood, *The Recovery of Family Life* (New York: Harper & Row, 1953), p. 190.

2. *Quote,* 68:300.

3. *Quote,* 66:515.

4. Lofton Hudson, *Home Is the Place* (Nashville: Broadman Press, 1967), p. 17.

5. Jack R. Taylor, *One Home Under God* (Nashville: Broadman Press, 1974), p. 37.

6. *Quote,* 68:185.

7. Harry Emerson Fosdick, *The Hope of the World* (New York: Harper & Brothers, 1933), p. 157.